Riots

Alan and Katharine Dures

Batsford Academic and Educational   London

First published 1985

Typeset by Tek-Art Ltd, Kent
and printed in Great Britain by
R J Acford
Chichester, Sussex
for the publishers
Batsford Academic and Educational,
an imprint of B. T. Batsford Ltd,
4 Fitzhardinge Street
London W1H 0AH

ISBN 0 7134 4350 2

ACKNOWLEDGMENT

The Author and Publishers would like to thank the following for their kind permission to reproduce copyright illustrations: BBC Hulton Picture Library: figs. 1, 2, 3, 4, 5, 7, 8, 9, 10, 11, 12, 13, 14, 15, 16, 17, 18, 20, 21, 22, 23, 24, 25, 26, 27, 28, 29, 30, 31, 32, 33, 34, 35, 36, 37, 38, 39, 40, 41, 42, 43, 44, 45, 46, 47; Pat Hodgson Library, fig. 6; Syndication International, figs. 50, 54; Topham Picture Library, figs. 48, 49, 51, 52, 53, 55, 56, 57, 58. Fig. 19 is from the Publishers' collection. The picture research was by Pat Hodgson.

Contents

The Illustrations

Introduction

The absence of political violence has often been seen as part of the British character. In general this seem to be the case, though it is truer of England alone than of Britain as a whole. There were good reasons for the relative stability in the eighteenth and nineteenth centuries, the most important being the freedom from foreign invasion. Nevertheless, the existence of popular disturbances on a wide scale has been increasingly recognized by historians in recent years. England was by no means the haven of moderation portrayed by the older textbooks. In fact, popular protest, often of a violent kind, was commonplace, especially in the eighteenth and nineteenth centuries. The term "riot" was defined by the Riot Act of 1715, which made it a felony if an unlawful assembly of twelve or more people failed to disperse within an hour of the Riot Act being read by a magistrate or other officer. In the following pages we trace the changing nature of riots from the relatively controlled and disciplined protests of the eighteenth-century food riots to the spontaneous violence of the alienated youth of some British cities in the 1980s.

1
Food Riots, 1700-1830

The Causes

Most riots in the eighteenth century were caused by rises in the price of food. For example, of 275 known disturbances in Britain between 1735 and 1800, some two-thirds were food riots. But though the food riot had become so common by the eighteenth century, its origin is by no means clear. There is no conclusive evidence of such disturbance before the 1520s, though this may reflect the absence of sources. In the sixteenth and seventeenth centuries high food prices led to violent protest, and a recent study by Wrightson and Walter identified forty incidents of food rioting between 1585 and 1660. Nevertheless, the authors conclude that the years of dearth in early modern England "were not marked by widespread rioting".

There were two main reasons for the relative absence of disturbance. Firstly, there was widespread agreement among all classes that food shortages were due not to human agency but to God: God punished man for his sins. For example, in the scarcity of 1595 one Nicholas Bownde blamed dearth "upon prevalence of sabbath breaking", while in 1629 an Essex magistrate argued that "the best cure [of poor harvests] rests in consideration of the cause of this evil which is . . . drunkenness". Secondly, even in the seventeenth century the majority of people were not totally dependent on buying food; a

proportion of the population was still partially self-sufficient and therefore not so vulnerable to changes in prices.

By the eighteenth century people were less likely to find a religious explanation for food shortages. Also by this time England had a well-developed trade in foodstuffs; self-sufficiency had gone. Grain was the most important item in this trade and the most important food in the diet of the majority of the

1 A baker. In rural areas throughout the eighteenth century most people baked their own bread but as food became more commercialized professional bakers appeared, even in the countryside, by the early nineteenth century.
▼

population. Bread used up a considerable proportion of a worker's budget. Rudé, one of the great authorities on eighteenth-century riots, has calculated that the London artisan spent about a quarter of his income on bread. A family of five, including one baby, would need 2.5 kg of bread per day. Increasingly in the eighteenth century the bread that was eaten was wheaten bread. In 1765 Charles Smith, a contemporary writer, estimated that almost two-thirds of the population ate wheaten bread, with the rest divided between rye, oats and barley bread. Oats, barley and rye were more important in the poorer areas of the West and North. The very poorest lived mainly on potatoes, but these people were a tiny minority in England.

Given the dependence on wheat of the vast majority of the population, it is hardly surprising that the pattern of food riots should be closely linked to the price of wheat. Wheat prices were generally higher in the second half of the eighteenth century than in the first. Between 1713 and 1764 the average price was 34s 11d per quarter (that is a quarter of a hundredweight, or about 12.7 kg) and consequently bread sold at 5d or 6d per loaf, (for a 1.8 kg loaf). In the second half of the eighteenth century the average wheat price was over 55s per quarter, while in 1800 it reached the frighteningly high peak of 128s. The early eighteenth century had seen the food riot become common, so much so that a Carmarthenshire correspondent to *The Gentleman's Magazine* of 1757 could complain:

> *If the legislature don't speedily use some method effectually to suppress the present spirit of rioting which is become general among the lower sort of people . . . there will be no protection from the plundering mob. The Mob must be conquered.*

But far from being conquered, the "mob" was more active in the second half of the eighteenth century. Following the pattern of grain prices, there were 40 incidents in 1766 alone and major riots in 1772, 1792-93, 1800,

The BRITISH-BUTCHER.
Supplying JOHN BULL with a Substitute for BREAD.

2 A comment on the high price of food in 1794 due to poor harvests and high taxation. High food prices and also the burden of recruitment to find men for the wars against France brought discontent throughout the decade.

1816 and 1824-30. This was primarily the result of a number of harvest failures in these years. But the upward movement of grain prices was due, more generally, to the increased population in England and Wales. This in turn resulted in England changing from being a net exporter of grain before the mid-eighteenth century, to becoming an importer. Between 1775 and 1786 some 2½% of the requirement of grain was imported, while in the first decade of the nineteenth century over 7½% of wheat was imported.

By the eighteenth century few people actually produced their own grain for consumption. Also by this time the chain between the consumer and the wheat grower had become a longer one. The growth of towns meant that an efficient marketing system had to be evolved, which included not only a merchant, but a professional miller and the transporting of grain over long distances. Not surprisingly, a substantial portion of all disturbances took place at ports, market towns or places from which grain was moved to another part of England. This helps to explain why East Anglia, which was the best wheat-growing area in the country, still had the most heavy concentration of riots. Its grain was frequently being moved, either by cart or by coastal vessel, to London. This caused indignation among the local population in times of shortage. In 1766, for example, several hundred townsmen rose in Colchester and stopped two wagons "loaded with meal" from being sent out of the town. Disorders were closely linked to communication networks in the shortages of 1795-96, when at least fifty food disturbances took place at communication centres. A number of riots in these years occurred at small ports, such as Seaford, Chichester, Wells, Boston and Wisbech. Others took place inland, at canal or river termini such as Bedford, Ipswich, Winchester and Lewes. Small market towns, especially those exporting grain to London, such as Hitchin, Halstead and Potters Bar, also suffered.

Riot Action

The purpose of food riots was usually to prevent food being moved, as we saw with Colchester, or to compel traders to reduce their wheat prices. This was the purpose of the rioters in Berkshire in July 1766:

Thomas Tames with a great number of otherly disorderly persons were at John Lyford the younger . . . and declared they were Regulators and would lower the Prices of Corn and swore they would be damn'd if they wou'd not take away his wheat and

threatened to break open his cottage if he wou'd not open the Doors.

G. Rudé, The Crowd in History

At Honiton in Devon the crowd took charge of trading, seizing "bags of corn lodged by the farmers in the public houses . . . and sold the corn at 5s 6d per bushel paying the money and returning the bags to the owners."

Mills were often a target for food rioters, since their owners were middlemen, who were often blamed for high prices. In Devon in 1765-66 there were several thousand rioters whose target was mills on which they inflicted more than £1000 worth of damage. At Norwich in 1766 a mob tore down a mill, threw flour into the river and destroyed furniture, plate and accounts. The mob often showed its fury or even contempt for the middleman by spoiling food, as in the Norwich incident, rather than by reselling it. So serious did the assaults on mills become, that when the Riot Act was extended in 1764, attacks on mills were made a felony and therefore a capital offence.

The great majority of disturbances were more ceremonial than today's riots. Mobs were often headed by someone beating a drum, blowing a horn or carrying a flag. The East Anglian crowds in 1816 marched under a banner inscribed "fife and drum". A loaf draped in black crêpe was the symbol of London rioters in 1816 when food shops were attacked. Other crowds wore ribbons, such as those who attacked carts near Newcastle-under-Lyme in 1800.

Large numbers of industrial workers took part in food riots. Cornish tinners, Staffordshire potters, West Country weavers, were all involved in such disturbances. Since more riots took place in market towns than in the country proper, agricultural workers were, in fact, less prominent than other groups. Women played an important part in food riots during this period. It was women who had to go to market to feed the family. At Dover in 1740, according to the *Ipswich Journal*, a crowd of women "rose in tumultuous manner, cut the sacks and took away the grain that the

3 The burning of Albion Mills, Blackfriars Bridge, 1791. The mills were popularly (and incorrectly) believed to raise the price of bread and they were the main target for food rioters.

farmers were bringing to the ports for shipping". Resenting the attempts to export corn when prices were high, these women pelted the teams and their drivers with stones for three miles out of town. In September 1800 the Mayor of Blandford Forum wrote to the Home Office, complaining that his house was surrounded by women demanding food at fair prices. Such was the involvement of women that the *Leicester Journal* of 12 September 1801 remarked that "all public disturbances generally commence with the clamour of women and the folly of boys".

Indirectly, soldiers could also play a significant part in riots, as in the disturbances of 1795-96. At this time, soldiers were encamped all along the east and south coast, to guard against a French invasion. On the east coast, at King's Lynn, the local authorities complained that 700 soldiers and their families were exhausting the town's supply of wheat. In South Devon in 1795 the outward-bound fleet of some 25,000 sailors was held up offshore for a number of weeks. A local correspondent pointed out that this was equivalent to the whole population of towns and villages in the area. Prices rose spectacularly. South Devon's wheat was 5s a quarter above the national average by 14 March and by April, 8s above. The result was an outbreak of rioting in towns of South Devon and the Tamar Valley, in which soldiers took an active part.

The riots of 1766 were some of the most typical and widespread of the eighteenth-century food riots. The wheat crop was poor in 1766, described by *The Gentleman's Magazine* as "much of it being smutty, much blighted, and very much choked with weeds". By September 1766, a correspondent wrote from East Anglia that "the crops of wheat were very bad in Norfolk and Suffolk, bad to a degree not known to us, nor perhaps to our forefathers".

Prices had already begun to rise in early summer, especially in the West Country. Between June and September 1766 prices of wheat at Gloucester went up almost 50%. Other foodstuffs were also going up in price. Butter, meat and cheese all became more expensive. At the Stourbridge Fair on 18 September, "cheese sold dearer than has been known". Not surprisingly, therefore, riots started in the West Country in the last week of July. By August, the counties of Berkshire and Buckinghamshire were involved, while Midland and East Anglian counties soon followed.

The disturbances followed the characteristic food riot pattern of the eighteenth century. Crowds were determined to prevent the export of grain. In the Midlands, the rioters made their way along the route to the inland port of Stratford-upon-Avon, stopping all the grain wagons on the way and selling their contents. In Lyme Regis, the mob blamed high prices on the export of grain from the port. Pressure, sometimes of a violent nature, was put on farmers and merchants to lower their prices. In October 1766, farmers at Alton in Hampshire were so alarmed by a threatening

letter, that "in great consternation they consented to lower the prices of provisions to the poor".

The greatest violence was characteristically shown to middlemen. At the end of October 1766, Norwich was the scene of violent action, with millers, bakers and other tradesmen the object of the crowd's anger.

A general insurrection began, when the proclamation [i.e. the Riot Act] was read in the market place, where provisions of all sorts were scattered about by rioters in heaps, the new mill, a spacious building, which supplied the city with water, was attacked and pulled down; the flour, to the number of 150 sacks thrown, sack after sack, into the river; the bakers' shops plundered and shattered; a large malt house set fire to and burnt; houses and warehouses pulled down; and the whole city thrown into the greatest confusion.

In the absence of military help close to hand, the Norwich magistrates "issued out a summons to the housekeepers in their respective districts to assemble with staves to oppose the rioters". The conflict was long and bloody, but in the end the rioters were overpowered. Following the defeat of the rioters, thirty were arrested, with eight subsequently suffering the death penalty. Reprisals generally were harsh; ninety were brought to trial at Gloucester, of whom nine were eventually hanged and a further seven

4 There were riots in East Anglia and London in 1816. Not only were banners carried as part of the ritual of riots, but loaves draped in black crêpe or smeared with blood also provided emblems for the rioters.

▼

transported. Both county militias and the military were used to disperse riots.

The rioters, however, did achieve some of their objectives. In late September 1766, King George III issued an order in Council, stating that no further wheat should be exported. Also, some magistrates and farmers decided on their own initiative to lower prices. A certain William Kelmarsh of Northamptonshire went to considerable trouble to help the situation. Hearing of riots in the Midlands while he was abroad, he purchased 100,000 quarters of wheat in Flanders, and returned to sell wheat at a modest price in his native Northamptonshire.

The main riots before the end of the century, 1772-73, 1783 and 1795-96, also conformed to the typical pattern of food disturbances, but fixed the price of butter and cheese as well as grain. In 1772 market towns were again to the fore. In April there was mob violence at Colchester, while in May, Bury St Edmunds experienced four days of rioting. The rioters obliged the:

meal men and shopkeepers to sell them their commodities at their own prices [i.e. prices fixed by rioters]. The dealers in Butter and Cheese were also visited by them and the price of their goods was fixed at 4¹/2d a pound for butter and 5d a pound for cheese.
R.F. Wearmouth,
Methodism and the Common
People

The town was in a similar position to Norwich in 1766, with no resident soldiers. As a result, "all the Inhabitants were under the most melancholy Apprehension of the Dangerous Consequences". Even the farmers were afraid and dared not bring "either Fowls, Butter or Eggs to the market". Eventually, the rioters were dispersed by "the vigorous action of a combined force of fifteen hundred tradesmen and inhabitants". The Bury disturbances also spread to surrounding villages. At Ixworth, the mob entered the premises of a local miller and "set him on the table and put him up for auction after which they drove him through the town beating him with sticks."

The Political Elements

The disturbances of 1799-1800 were similar to earlier food riots in many respects, but there were also differences. The causes of violence were undoubtedly the deficient harvest and high prices of the time. In May 1801, William Rowbottom noted that "a great deal of families have sold their household goods to exist". As in previous riots, there were frequent reports of attempts to prevent the movement of food. Barges were stopped on the Aire and Calder canals taking grain to Leeds and Bradford.

In the 1800 incidents, however, there was the suggestion of a political element, absent in previous bread riots. Jacobin agitators, (supporters of the French Revolution) were widely blamed. J. Westcomb Emmerton noted that the poor of Nottinghamshire were:

not at all inclined to belief that there is a deficiency in last year's crop and the Jacobites, who are for taking advantage of the times, encourage that notion.

The historian E.P. Thompson has argued that in the 1790s there was considerable revolutionary activity in England. He has seen the outbreaks of 1799-1800 as examples of this revolutionary tradition. In fact, it is difficult to link these disturbances with actions in France and radical politics in general. Not a single British Jacobin or French agent was arrested, and most riots appear to have been in spontaneous reaction to rising food prices.

The language of the rioters, however, was certainly influenced by the French Revolution, and in some disturbances, political slogans were prominent. One anonymous versifier in Essex sent this message to the farmers and magistrates:

On Swill and Grain you wish the poor to be fed,

And underneath the Guilliotine we could wish to see your heads.

Another circular from Somerset addressed itself to "half Starv'd Britons":

*Then raise ye drooping spirits up
Nor starve by Pitt's decree
Fix up the sacred Guillotine
Proclaim – French Liberty!*

Just outside Sheffield in December 1800 there were national meetings of discontented people. It was reported that some of the crowd had used revolutionary language. They had advocated striking at:

the root of evil, namely the government; Mr Pitt and all his measures were execrable to Human Nature. Nothing could prosper in present hands . . . .
    C. Emsley, British Society and the French Wars

There is no evidence, however, that such inflammatory language got near to being turned into revolutionary action.

Food riots were the main form of protest by labourers and craftsmen in the eighteenth century. They were a form of "collective bargaining" aimed at achieving a "natural justice", especially fairer food prices. The food riots were less violent than urban disturbances of the eighteenth century or later rural protests. Property was more of a target than people, and rioters were more likely to be killed than farmers or millers. But farmers and millers were usually treated differently. Rioters would often seize food from farmers, sell it at lower prices and give the money back to the farmers. At mills there was likely to be the highest level of destruction, with grain wasted and buildings attacked. This reflected the bitter feelings of many labourers and craftsmen that middlemen such as millers were responsible for high food prices. By the early nineteenth century, strike action and demands for higher wages were beginning to replace food riots as the major form of bargaining. Also, the growth of industry and the fact that after 1815 people started to demand the reform of parliament led to greater violence.

5 By the nineteenth century the nature of rural riots was changing, and they were likely to be more violent. One of the most common acts of violence against farmers by labourers was the burning of ricks, as we see here on a Kent farm in 1830.
▼

2
Eighteenth-Century Urban Riots

London was by far the most important urban centre for riots in the eighteenth century, as indeed it had been in the late seventeenth. Disturbances in the capital were not usually caused by high food prices. George Rudé, the historian of riots, has commented that:

There was not in London – as there was in English rural districts, and for that matter, in Paris, before and during the Revolution – a close general concordance betwen high food price and popular disturbances.

The absence of food riots was due mainly to London's favoured position in the grain trade, with the capital drawing wheat from all the southern and eastern counties, and also to the close watch kept by London magistrates on the prices of foodstuffs. London riots were caused primarily by political and religious factors. Religious riots often involved racial issues as

6 Election riots were a common cause of disorder throughout the eighteenth and nineteenth centuries. Though only the landed gentry had the vote in the eighteenth century, urban elections especially provided opportunities for the crowds to express their views forcefully. Elections offered good popular entertainment in an age when amusements were few.
▼

well. These disturbances, especially the religious ones, were less restrained than food riots.

The Sacheverell Disturbances

The most serious disturbances in London in the early decades of the eighteenth century were those in support of the High Church Tory, Dr Henry Sacheverell. By the late seventeenth century, Protestant Nonconformists, such as Presbyterians, had a good measure of religious toleration and had built their own chapels in London and elsewhere. The Act of 1689 had given toleration to such "dissenters", and by the early eighteenth century there were one million Nonconformists in England, of whom 100,000 lived in London, especially in Westminster and Southwark. This development was resented by those who supported the Anglican Church. Dr Sacheverell was a staunch Anglican. He was also an opponent of the then governing party, the Whigs. By 1710, there was increasing hostility to the Whigs, who were blamed for the continuation of the War of the Spanish Succession. Opponents of the Whigs believed that Whig financiers were profiting from the war by lending money to the government. Also, Nonconformists were believed to be ardent supporters of the Whig government. With the smaller merchants and artisans in London forced to pay increased taxes for the war, and discontent heightened by high prices in 1709, Whigs and Nonconformists became the main targets for criticism.

On 5 November 1709, Dr Sacheverell refused to deliver the usual type of sermon preached on Guy Fawkes' Day (sacred to the Whigs as the day on which England had been delivered from Popery) and instead attacked Nonconformists (dissenters) using St Paul's text, "In perils among false brethren". The printed version of the sermon was widely circulated, forcing the Whig government to take action. On 14 December, a complaint was made to the House of Commons, where Sacheverell's sermon was denounced as a

7 Henry Sacheverell. Support for the High Church Tory Dr Sacheverell was the cause of the 1710 riots in London. In a sermon preached at St Paul's on the text "In perils amongst false brethren" Sacheverell condemned religious toleration and attacked the Whig government. His arrest led to the riots.

"malicious, scandalous and seditious libel". Both he and his publisher, Henry Clements, were summoned to attend the Bar of the House of Commons. The trial was then moved to Westminster Hall, where it began on 27 February and lasted for three weeks.

Long before the trial was completed, indeed on the night of 1-2 March 1710, London erupted with cries of "Sacheverell and Church for ever". The first goal of the mob was the rich Presbyterian meeting house south of Lincoln's Inn Fields. The crowd chanted "Down with the Bank of England and Meeting Houses, and God damn the Presbyterians and all that support them" – showing their hatred of both dissenters and money men. Much of London's West End was occupied by Sacheverell's supporters, who stopped frightened citizens, saying, "God damn you, are you for the doctor?"

The dissenting Nonconformist chapels, however, were the only real targets, with the six best-known destroyed in one night. John Dyer, writer of the best-selling Tory newsletter, recorded:

They burnt not only the joiners' work of these meeting houses, which they destroyed, but also fine clocks, brass benches and chairs and cushions of the vestry rooms; and they seized the builder of that in Leather Lane and threatened to throw him into the fire alleging his crime was very great, for by building such houses he drew people from public worship of God in the National Church.

Though Londoners on that night in 1710 were, no doubt, terrified by the mob, the rioters in fact were quite disciplined and their targets carefully planned. They avoided destroying any property other than dissenting chapels, while they often carried furnishings a considerable distance away, to burn them safely in an open space or broad street. When the rioters arrived at the chapels, they were already equipped with their tools of destruction, such as crow bars, pick axes, smiths' hammers and woodmen's axes. In fact, the demolition of the chapels, without endangering themselves or other citizens, suggests a high degree of organization.

The disciplined nature of the riot is confirmed by an analysis of those who took part. The rioters were not the unemployed and poorest sections of London society, but included two lawyers, a former banker and a physician, as well as a large number of apprentices. Indeed, Professor Holmes has commented that:

These rioters must have been some of the most "respectable" of the eighteenth century; the great majority were fully employed and several were self-employed tradesmen or professional men.

There must be a strong suspicion, though it is impossible to prove, that some of the magistrates in London with strong Anglican and Tory sentiments turned a blind eye to the riots. There was strong support for Dr Sacheverell in high places. For example, Sir Samuel Gerrard, elected Mayor of London in 1710, had congratulated Sacheverell on the sermon for which he was eventually tried.

Few people suffered injury in the 1710 riots. The only casualties were among the rioters themselves, two of whom died and fifty of whom were wounded, several of them suffering no more than cuts from splintering glass. The relatively small number of casualties was due not only to the disciplined nature of the mob but also to the action of the authorities. Some crack troops were used for riot control, such as the Life and Coldstream Guards and the Second Horse Grenadiers, which included a high proportion of soldiers experienced in Marlborough's campaigns.

Another significant factor was the absence of a Riot Act, which was to be passed in 1715. Up to 1715, professional troops and militiamen alike had to be very careful of killing or maiming. Soldiers could be taken to court for their action if any victim was subsequently shown to be innocent of riot. Moreover, even if they killed a rioter, they could be charged with murder if it could be shown that they had used force in excess of what was necessary to keep the peace. Consequently, the troops rarely opened fire; in three hours' patrolling of Lincoln's Inn and Drury Lane at the height of the riots, the troops did not fire a single shot.

Anti-Irish Disturbances

The 1736 riot in London was probably the first in which a racial issue, anti-Irish feeling in this case, was a major factor. The disturbances began as a dispute over the employment of Irish labour in the east London parishes of Shoreditch and Spitalfields, spreading later to Whitechapel. A master builder, William Goswell, who was in charge of rebuilding St

Leonard's Church in Shoreditch, dismissed a number of English labourers who wanted higher pay. In their place, he took on Irishmen at between one half and two-thirds of the English labourers' pay. This brought to a head anti-Irish feeling in a number of London parishes. A large amount of Irish labour was already employed in the weaving industry in Shoreditch and Spitalfields. English labourers feared for their jobs and rates of pay.

A crowd of disgruntled English labourers began to assemble at Shoreditch on the evening of Monday, 26 July 1736, shouting "Down with the Irish!" But their numbers were not great that night and they soon dispersed. Sir Robert Walpole wrote to the Prime Minister, his brother Horace:

> *On Tuesday evening they assembled again in bodies, and about 7 o'clock were thought to be 2,000 in number. They now grew more riotous; they attacked a public house kept by an Irishman, broke down all the doors and windows and quite gutted the house. Another house of the same sort underwent the same fate . . . .*

The crowd rose to some 4,000 that night, but soon dispersed when the Guards were called. Though there were further attacks on Irish property, the troubles were over by the end of July. Though, by later standards, damage was slight, with half a dozen Irish houses smashed, the significance of the riot lies in its racialism. The anti-Irish sentiment, together with a strong anti-Catholic feeling, was to surface again in a powerful form in the Gordon riots.

Wilkes and Liberty

The hostility of the City of London to George III and his favourite Lord Bute, in the early 1760s, forms the background to the Wilkes disturbances. By the mid-eighteenth century, the City of London was developing a distinctive political character of its own. Radicals in the City began to formulate a programme of reform, including the demand

8 John Wilkes first came to prominence in 1763, when he was already MP for Aylesbury and aged 36. He denounced George III's speech arguing for peace with France in 1863 in the famous issue no. 45 of *North Briton.*

for shorter parliaments and the giving of the vote to a wider range of people. This issue attracted the support of many London artisans. Wilkes became one of the most important spokesmen of this new City radicalism. His cause was also helped by a background of industrial disputes in London. The 1760s have been called by J.W. Shelton "the most remarkable decade of industrial disputes for over a century" and these disputes contributed to the climate of discontent.

In 1763, John Wilkes was already MP for Aylesbury. In that year he issued a newspaper, No.45 of *North Briton*, in which he denounced the King's speech and the peace terms ending the Seven Years' War with France. He was committed to the Tower on a charge of libel. He was released a week later by Chief Justice Pratt, who declared that Wilkes's arrest was a breach of parliamentary privilege. On his release from prison, Wilkes was escorted to his house by a large crowd shouting "Wilkes and Liberty!" He was already showing his considerable ability as a leader. He managed to identify his plea for "Liberty" with the

9 In 1763 Wilkes was arrested on a general warrant following the publication of no. 45 of *North Briton*. Lord Chief Justice Pratt declared the warrant a breach of parliamentary privilege. Wilkes managed to persuade "the middling and inferior sort of people" that his cause was also theirs, and on his return to London in 1768 he was a popular hero.

grievances of the craftsmen and lower middle classes in the capital.

Wilkes left the country in 1763, to avoid a charge of blasphemy because of another of his publications called *Essay on Women*. Returning in 1768, he was elected MP for Middlesex amidst great popular rejoicing. Mobs criss-crossed London from east to west, celebrating Wilkes's victory. *No.45* was chalked on walls and doors and the Austrian Ambassador was dragged from his coach, just for the sport. The crowd ended up before the Mansion House, to settle accounts with Thomas Harley, the Lord Mayor, an opponent of Wilkes. To shouts of "Wilkes for ever", they broke every lamp and window in the building. The Mansion House accounts record that damages to lamps amounted to £30 4s and to windows £174. Wilkes then gave himself up to the authorities and was imprisoned in the King's Bench for his obscene publication of 1763.

Wilkes commanded as much attention in prison as out of it. Large crowds assembled daily outside the King's Bench prison in Southwark. On 8 May 1768 the press reported that a "numerous Mob assembled about the King's Bench prison exclaiming against the confinement of Mr Wilkes". Wilkes watched from his cell window, made a brief speech and persuaded the crowd to disperse. But, before

they did so,

a well dressed man said to be a North Briton – probably an innocent passer-by – had been thrown into the pond for speaking offensively of Wilkes and made to get on his knees and shout "Wilkes and Liberty!".

The most violent incidents connected with the Wilkes affair occurred on 10 May 1768. This was the day parliament met, so the crowd gathered once more to demand Wilkes's release from prison to enable him to take up his seat in the Commons. The Southwark magistrates, expecting trouble, had ordered a troop of 100 men and horse of the Third Regiment of Foot Guards to guard the prison. Between 10 and 11 o'clock in the morning the Southwark magistrates received an urgent appeal for help from the prison marshal. Hurrying to the prison, they were greeted by cries of "No Wilkes, no King!", "Damn the King, damn the Government, damn the Justices!" and "This is the most glorious opportunity for a Revolution that ever offered!"

Justice Gillam felt obliged to read the Riot Act, which was met with jeers and a volley of stones. Gillam himself was struck. The military were ordered to catch the culprit; they bungled the job, managing instead to shoot a young cowman, William Allen. Allen almost certainly had nothing to do with the demonstration. Later the same afternoon, Gillam ordered the troops to fire into the crowd and "5 or 6 were killed on the spot and about 15 wounded". A number of people killed or wounded on that day were entirely innocent of riot, a point seized upon for propaganda purposes by the news-sheet *English Liberty*. This listed "some persons killed and wounded":

Mr William Allen, *shot to death in his father's cow house.*

Mr William Redburn, *weaver, shot through the thigh, died in London hospital.*

William Bridgeman, *shot through the breast as he was fitting a hay-cart in the Haymarket, died instantly.*

Mary Jeffs, *of St Saviour's, who was selling oranges by the Haymarket, died instantly.*

10 Wilkes was the major figure whose name was linked to most London riots in the 1760s and 1770s. After his election as mayor in 1773 his radicalism declined, and by 1779 he had dropped out of politics.
▼

The "massacre" of St George's Fields, as these incidents were known, proved to be the high point of pro-Wilkes demonstrations. The rioters killed no one. The troops were responsible for all the deaths. In a much lower key, the Wilkes-ite issues rumbled on for a number of years. Wilkes was elected no fewer than four times for Middlesex between 1768 and 13 April 1769, without being allowed to take up his seat. His fourth election provoked support from several thousand demonstrators, but the demonstrations were peaceful. Sporadic outbreaks for Wilkes continued until 1773. In that year, Wilkes became Lord Mayor, an event greeted with widespread rejoicing. In December he even regained his seat in parliament, and by the end of the decade he had dropped out of radical politics.

Industrial disputes had formed an important backcloth to Wilkes's radical politics. The coal-heavers' strike, which took place in the crucial year of 1768, was in fact more violent than any demonstration in favour of Wilkes. Coal-heavers unloaded coals from ships in the East End docks. They were employed by men known as "undertakers", who were also frequently publicans. In 1768 the coal-heavers went on strike. One undertaker, also a publican, John Green, of the Round About Tavern, Shadwell, became an object of hatred among the coal-heavers when he offered attractive wages to would-be strike-breakers. On 21 April 1768, a gang attacked Green's pub at about 8 p.m. with cries of "Wilkes and Liberty!" Green, with the assistance of his sister and a sailor, set about defending his tavern with musket fire, killing several coal-heavers. The mob responded by fetching muskets, and riddling the tavern with bullets. During the night, Green escaped over the rooftops. The rioters eventually broke into the inn with cries of "Green you bouger why don't you fire!" saying that they would "have his heart and liver" and "cut him to pieces and hang him upon his sign". Finding that Green had escaped, the crowd dragged his sister from the house and murdered her in the street. Seven coal-heavers were hanged.

Green and the sailor were also charged with murder, but acquitted.

The Gordon Riots

The Gordon riots of 1780 were the most serious of the eighteenth century. The disturbance was the largest since the Monmouth Rebellion of 1684, while no disorder since has led to more bloodshed or greater destruction of property. More people were killed or executed than in the subsequent Luddite violence, the Reform riots or various Chartist troubles. The source of the problem was a Catholic Relief Act passed in 1778, which repealed a number of restrictions imposed on Roman Catholics. It was not a radical measure; there was little resistance to the Bill in a still very Protestant House of Commons. Attempts to apply the Act in Scotland, however, provoked rioting in Glasgow, Edinburgh and smaller Scottish towns. In the face of such opposition, the British government abandoned the Act in Scotland. This encouraged the opponents of the Catholic Relief Act in England to campaign for its repeal. In February 1779, therefore, a Protestant Association in London was formed as a pressure group for the repeal of the Catholic Relief Act.

Lord George Gordon, who had already been active in the Scottish movements, became president of the English Association. Lord George was a young man of twenty-eight, but already an MP of five years' standing for a Wiltshire pocket borough. He was keen to further his political career by leading a popular campaign and the theme of "No Popery" played into his hands. On 25 November 1779, he spoke on the subject to the House of Commons.

The indulgences given to Papists have alarmed the whole country, and they [opponents of the Act] are determined with the utmost resolution to guard against a people that are become favourites in the eyes of the Ministry. I do not deliver my own sentiments only; government will find

120,000 men at my back who will avow and support them.

By January 1780 a campaign was under way to petition the House of Commons against Catholic Relief. The Protestant Association met in the Clothmakers' Hall on 29 May 1780 to discuss the best way to present a petition which had grown to over 100,000 signatures. Lord Gordon insisted on a mass demonstration to accompany it. Unless 20,000 at least attended outside parliament, he said that he would not present the petition. He pledged that for his part "he would run all hazards with the people, and if the people were too lukewarm to run all hazards with him, they might get another President".

Plans were made for the Protestant Association to meet in St George's Fields, Southwark, on 2 June, after which they would accompany Lord Gordon to the House of Commons to present the petition. The Association should assemble in four divisions for good order, each member should wear a blue ribbon and magistrates were invited to deal with any fringe troublemakers. Hibbert, in a recent history of the riots, describes the scene on that Friday morning.

When Lord George arrived just before eleven the crowd was loudly singing a good protestant hymn and at the sight of his coach cheer upon cheer could be heard above the din of the singing. As soon as he began to speak, the singing died down and conversation faded to a murmur. Lord George was anxious to impress upon them the need for restraint. They moved off to the skirl of bagpipes.

They moved towards Westminster, using four different bridges. The section crossing by Westminster Bridge was headed by a man carrying on his shoulder the great parchment roll containing over 100,000 signatures.

On reaching the Commons in the afternoon, Lord Gordon informed the Commons that he had a petition containing 120,000 signatures

against Catholic Relief and moved for a debate on the motion. His supporters had surrounded parliament. Lord George frequently left the House to address his followers, giving them news of the debates, including names of those opposing the petition. Many MPs were angered by Lord George's conduct, none more so than Colonel Holroyd, who warned him:

My Lord George, do you intend to bring your rascally adherents into the House of Commons? If you do, the first man of them that enters, I will plunge my sword not in his, but in your body.

Other MPs also threatened Lord George should the mob enter the House of Commons. Debate on the petition was adjourned till the following Tuesday. Most of the crowd gradually moved away from the Commons, but guards were needed to allow MPs out of the House at 11 p.m.

The crowd, however, was determined to have some sport, and a section of it moved from the Commons to attack Catholic property. The first targets were the Catholic embassy chapels in London. The chapel of the Sardinian Embassy in Duke Street, Lincoln's Inn Fields, was attacked, followed by the Bavarian Embassy in Warwick Street, St James's. The Sardinian chapel was burned to the ground. The mob then moved into Moorfields, where there was a large Irish population, but troops intervened and several rioters were arrested. This was the first violence of the riot. The weekend was relatively quiet, though on Monday a large crowd paraded in front of Gordon's house, showing off some of their trophies such as pulpits from Catholic chapels.

On Tuesday, 6 June, the House of Commons reassembled to discuss the petition against Catholic Relief. Crowds again assembled outside parliament. At 5 o'clock Justice Hyde read the Riot Act and ordered the Horse Guards to disperse these crowds. One of the crowd hoisted a red flag and with cries of "To Hyde's house a hoy!" the mob moved towards St Martin's Street to punish Justice Hyde for his actions. They sacked Hyde's house, and burnt its contents in street bonfires. A neighbour of Hyde's described the scene:

There were six of these fires. Such a scene I have never before beheld. As it grew dusk, the wretches who were involved with smoke and covered with dust, flames glowing upon them like so many infernals. . . . At last the ringleaders gave the word and away they ran past our windows to the bottom of Lincoln's Inn Fields, with lighted firebrands in their hands like so many furies.

G. Hibbert, The Gordon Riots

Wednesday, 7 June, "Black Wednesday", saw the climax of the riots. Two attacks were made on the Bank of England, but were repulsed. King's Bench and Fleet prisons were set alight. Horace Walpole wrote on 8 June that "Unless I have a very bad memory, I never till last night saw London and Southwark in flames." The most spectacular event was the attack on a wealthy Catholic distiller, Thomas Langdale. At dusk, his premises were fired,

with the great vats of liquor igniting, and the fire spreading to twenty houses. A number of the rioters, already drunk from the gin given to them by Langdale to hold them at bay, tried to loot the burning buildings and were killed. Men, women and children were observed drinking the burning alcohol as it ran down the gutters.

All during the week, the number of troops in the capital had been increasing. By "Black Wednesday", there were several thousand. Regiments were rushed in from other parts of the country; the Northumberland Militia made a forced march of twenty-five miles to arrive in time to defend the Bank of England. Hyde Park was turned into a military camp because of the shortage of barracks. By Thursday, 8 June, with 10,000 troops in London, the riots were dying out. Lord George Gordon, who had been trying unsuccessfully to control his followers since Tuesday evening, was arrested on Friday, 9 June. He was taken from his house in Welbeck Street and placed in the Tower.

Not surprisingly, the cost of the riots was considerable. 210 people were killed outright, with 75 subsequent deaths, mostly rioters. 405 rioters were arrested, 62 were sentenced to death, but only 25 were finally hanged.

11 Troops massed in London streets during the Gordon riots. About 10,000 troops were used in the capital in addition to the militia and armed volunteers.
▼

Damage to buildings was estimated at £100,000. By any criteria, these were the worst riots of the eighteenth century. In spite of the appalling destruction of life and property, the riots also had some of the characteristics of discipline and organization noticeable in both the grain riots and the Sacheverell disturbances. The riots represented a cross-section of London workers and "do not appear, in the main, to have belonged to the very poorest sections of the working population" (Professor Rudé's verdict). Though pickpockets and thieves joined the violence, the main body of rioters had clear objectives. Initially, the disturbances were sparked off by traditional

12 Although the Gordon riots were caused by hatred of Catholicism, the symbols of authority such as prisons and the houses of judges and magistrates were targets for the rioters. Here the rioters are burning Newgate gaol.

▼

anti-Catholic feeling, tinged with hatred of foreigners, especially the Irish. But as the violence spread, it is noticeable that attacks tended to be made on the wealthy, rather than the poorer, Catholics. Symbols of authority were also targets – such as prisons, the Bank of England and the houses of magistrates.

There is strong evidence to suggest that at most times the mob was not involved in indiscriminate destruction. As with the Sacheverell riot, there was considerable discipline. Horace Walpole commented on this:

One strange circumstance in the late delirium was the mixture of rage and consideration. In most of the fires the mob threw furniture into the streets, did not burn it in *the house: nay they made several bonfires lest a small one should spread to buildings. They would not suffer [fire] engines to play on the devoted edifices; yet,*

the moment the objects were consumed, played engines on contiguous houses on each side.

The riots would not have taken place without the leadership of Lord George Gordon and the Protestant Association. Lord George tried to use the mob as an extra-parliamentary force; to many London workmen he seemed to legitimize violence and to provide an opportunity to attack the rich. As with the Sacheverell riots, there must be the suspicion that, at first, the City of London politicians gave the riots tacit support. Several London MPs sympathized with the Protestant Association and Lord George Gordon lodged with one Alderman Bull during the riots. The Common Council of London actually passed a resolution against Catholic Relief when the riots were taking place. This was regarded by some contemporaries as encouragement to the Protestant mob. Some London magistrates seemed to be slow to take action against the rioters.

The Gordon riots had one significant political consequence. After 1780, the close connection between the London mob and radical politicians in London, such as Wilkes, was broken. The governing classes had found themselves faced with mob rule of the worst kind. Thereafter, only the most desperate or foolish would risk trying to use the mob for its own cause. Lord George Gordon had shown how easily such tactics could backfire.

Conclusion

Urban riots in the eighteenth century were mainly centred on London. As the capital and centre of government, London was the most likely place for political demonstrations. It had the largest number of foreign citizens and racial issues were present in many eighteenth-century riots. Urban riots were more likely to be violent than rural disturbances; rural riots tended to focus on one issue – the price of food – whereas urban riots often brought in issues other than the main immediate cause of the disturbance. In both the Wilkes and Lord Gordon riots class conflict operated alongside the main political and religious issues. Both types of riot, however, had a strong sense of organization and discipline, and this was the outstanding characteristic of the eighteenth-century riot.

3
Decades of Violence, 1800-1850

By the early nineteenth century, the pattern of riots was changing. The main instrument of change was the Industrial Revolution. Industrial disputes, which had made only minor contributions to violence in the eighteenth century, began to replace food riots as the major cause of disturbance. Trade slumps replaced high food prices as the main cause of riot. London remained an important centre of protest, but urban disturbances were also to be found in the emerging industrial towns of the North and the Midlands. The increased class conflict that followed industrialization meant that the ruling classes were less likely to give the tacit support to riots that they had sometimes given before. Moreover, the degree of violence resulting from the Gordon riots had made the respectable classes wary of trying to use riot for their own ends.

The one exception was the political agitation for changes to the voting system. Up to 1832, the middle-class supporters of parliamentary reform and the political radicals canvassed working-class support, and

though they did not advocate violence, they had, on occasions, to tolerate it. Rural riots also changed. Food riots were giving way to disturbances concerned with wages. The most violent rural protest of the period, the Swing riots of 1830, focused their hatred on the new threshing machines. The countryside was thus affected by industrial change in the early nineteenth century and agricultural protest was brought more in line with industrial disputes. It is also significant that with increasing urbanization in the nineteenth

13 Talk of insurrection was in the air in 1817, with ➤ conspiracies in London, the North and the Midlands. The only actual rising was the Pentrick rising near Nottingham led by Jeremiah Brandreth, a twenty-seven-year old man who had worked a number of trades and had only recently moved into the area. Brandreth was executed along with two others, while thirty more were transported.

century, rural riots became less frequent after the 1830s.

The Luddite Riots

The Luddite riots were typical of the troubled years of the early nineteenth century. The name Luddite was said to have originated from a certain Ned Ludlam, a Leicester stockinger's apprentice who smashed his master's frames with a hammer after being reprimanded for some misdemeanour. Three features mark out the Luddite disturbances as different from most eighteenth-century riots. The areas concerned were mainly the industrial areas of the Midlands and the North, stretching from Leicester to York. The principal targets for the rioters were machines, especially new ones, in the textile industry. The disturbances were also remarkably destructive, provoking a strong response from the government. At the height of the trouble in the summer of 1812 there

14 The Riot Act was first passed in 1715. Once it was read to the assembled crowd the military could take action without fear of being sued for causing injury or even death.

were more than 12,000 troops stationed in the affected areas. This was a larger force than Wellington took to Portugal in the Peninsula War in 1808. Damage to machinery and property amounted to over £100,000.

Three main trade and geographical areas were affected: the framework knitting industry in Nottinghamshire, Leicestershire and Derbyshire; the woollen industry in Yorkshire; and the cotton trade in Lancashire and Cheshire. In the knitting trade it was mainly the frames used for the production of hosiery and lace that were attacked. In Yorkshire the main targets for the rioters were the shearing gigs which were replacing hand-shearing in the woollen industry. In the cotton industry power looms, which were making hand-loom weavers redundant, were destroyed.

15 In the troubled decade of 1840-50 there were many riots among the industrial workers. Here cotton operatives attack a mill in Preston but are repulsed by the military, with the magistrate on horseback reading the Riot Act.

16 The Luddite riots, 1811. This caricature portrays the leader of the Luddites as a woman. This was intended to be disparaging as no-one knew the real identity of "King Lud".

Though new machinery was the target for the riots, the cause of the outbreaks was the disastrous state of trade in 1811. British exports to North America had fallen from £11 million worth of goods in 1810 to £2 million in 1811. This particularly hit the framework knitting trade of the East Midlands. In March 1811 a number of employers in the knitting industry tried to lower wages, but with food prices at a very high level, the stockingers refused to accept this. A large group of stockingers gathered in Nottingham market place in March 1811 demanding "a more liberal price" for their work. That evening, more than sixty frames belonging to the hosiers who refused to pay "liberal wages" were smashed throughout Nottingham. More widespread and serious attacks occurred in November as violence spread to Leicestershire and Derbyshire. Between March 1811 and February 1812 it has been estimated that over 1,000 frames were destroyed in a hundred different attacks.

In Lancashire and Cheshire, where the major industry was cotton, the power loom was the object of the rioters' hatred. A Stockport warehouse owned by William Ratcliffe, the inventor of a new power loom, was attacked on 20 March 1812. Large numbers of weavers were, according to reports, sworn into secret societies in villages between Bolton and Manchester. Weavers were also present, along with colliers and carters, on 21 April 1812, in an attack on a steam loom belonging to a Mr

Burton living near Middleton, in Lancashire. The crowd was armed with "muskets and fixed bayonets, and others with colliers' picks marched to Middleton headed by a *Man of Straw* representing the renowned General Ludd whose standard bearer waved a sort of red flag." Mr Burton's mill was destroyed, with five attackers killed and eighteen injured.

The most significant aspect of Luddism was its scale. The events we have examined were only part of a more widespread reaction to a rapidly changing pattern of textile manufacture as steam power threatened to make groups like the hand-loom weavers redundant. At the same time as the Luddite riots, the Scottish weavers were involved in some of the most serious strikes of the early nineteenth century, with 40,000 looms idle for six weeks. Depite the new aspects of the Luddite riots, there was a continuity with earlier disturbances. The machine breakers saw themselves as an "Army of Redress". Their letters show that they felt that they were dispensing justice rather than breaking the law. Thus, in this sense, they were still in the eighteenth-century tradition of "collective bargaining by riot".

The Passing of the Corn Laws

Despite the growth of towns in the Midlands and the North, London was still a focus for many protests in the early nineteenth century. The passing of the Corn Laws in 1815, for example, created scenes reminiscent of the Gordon riots. The Corn Laws prohibited the import of foreign wheat until home-grown wheat reached 80s a quarter (hundredweight). This was good for British landowners, but not for the consumers of bread. The *London Chronicle* made this point in March 1815:

> *This question is now brought to an issue between the owners of land on the one hand and all the rest of the community who do not derive their income from the land . . .*

On the third reading of the Bill, 10-20,000

17 1846: while many of the working class were involved in mass demonstrations in the 1840s, the essentially middle class Anti-Corn Law League used more peaceful methods. Because of their greater power, petitioning was more successful for the Anti-Corn Law League than for the Chartists.

people assembled outside the Commons. Once dispersed by the military, the crowd attacked houses of the leading supporters of the Bill. Frederick Robinson, the mover of the Bill, was a particular target. His effigy was found hanging from a tree in Islington with the words "this is the post of honour for those who support the Corn Laws". In spite of a petition from Westminster signed by 42,473 people and a number of threatening letters sent to the lawyers who had drawn up the Bill, the Corn Laws were passed without further violence.

The Demand for Parliamentary Reform

The ending of the Napoleonic Wars brought

severe economic problems to the country. In London, unemployment rose sharply because of a decline in trade by 1816 and the release of the armed forces brought more destitute into London. With the end of the wars, the demand for parliamentary reform revived strongly, so that the post-1815 violence had a strongly political element. Though most radicals supporting the reform cause denounced violence, certain extreme left-wing groups such as the Spenceans, who were to address a large meeting in Spa Fields on 2 December 1816, along with other supporters of reform, were planning violent action. Three days before the meeting, Home Office spies had told the government of revolutionary plans by the Spenceans. These included plans to "Burn and destroy all jails in the Metropolis and let out the prisoners" and "seize arms belonging to the Honourable Artillery Regiment". Although the government made elaborate preparations for 2 December, for the Spa Fields meeting, a crowd of 200 Spencean supporters left the main meeting and made for the Tower of London. It took two hours for the cavalry to disperse the crowd, by which time they had seized over 200 muskets in the area around the Tower. If the crowd had but known it, the Tower was without ammunition until the late evening and a determined attack on the Tower might well have been successful.

It is difficult to know whether the attack on the Tower was part of a well-laid plan or a spontaneous rising. Certainly, Home Secretary Sidmouth had been given information that radicals in the provinces were expecting a signal to start a rising. On the other hand, Henry Hunt, the main speaker at the Spa Fields meeting, condemned the Spenceans for "their disgraceful and contemptible riot". Sidmouth remained convinced that revolutionary conspiracy might be successful because of the severe economic problems, especially in the textile areas. In February 1820 Arthur Thistlewood, a participant at Spa Fields, planned to assassinate the Cabinet in the so-called Cato Street Conspiracy. This incident has often been dismissed as isolated and pathetic, but it may have been part of a wider plan of

18 The Cato Street Conspiracy. Arthur Thistlewood and his fellow conspirators are pounced upon in a room in Cato Street, London. The government knew all about their plans to assassinate the Cabinet when attending dinner at Lord Harrowby's, because of a spy, George Edwards.

▼

19 Henry Hunt was one of the most famous radicals of his day, and he toured the country addressing meetings in support of parliamentary reform. Here we see him in St Peter's Square, Manchester in 1816.

disturbance. On 4 March 1820, Sidmouth wrote that:

> an expectation prevailed among the disaffected in the northern parts of the kingdom that an important blow would be struck in London, previous to expiration of the month of February.

There were rumours of a widespread rising in the manufacturing districts, and Sidmouth believed that the weaving centres of Leeds, Manchester, Carlisle and Glasgow would be implicated.

The Peterloo Massacre

Though such revolutionary groups as the Spenceans were a minority, agitation for parliamentary reform was widespread. One of the largest crowds assembled to demonstrate for reform was in St Peter's Fields, Manchester on 16 August 1819. By late morning some 60,000 people had assembled, and the Manchester magistrates were alarmed by the size of the crowd. When Henry Hunt arrived to address the crowd at 1 o'clock, the magistrates declared "that the whole bore the appearance of insurrection", though in fact no disturbance had occurred. Forty yeomen cavalry were sent into the assembled thousands to arrest Hunt. This was duly done, but the yeomanry then found themselves trapped within the crowd. The magistrates therefore decided to send in the Hussars. In panic, people began to flee; many were trapped; others beaten down or slashed with swords. Eleven people were killed and 400 injured within the space of fifteen minutes in what came to be known as the "Peterloo" massacre.

The government had little option other than to support the magistrates publicly; in private, the Prime Minister, Lord Liverpool, admitted that the magistrates had acted "injudiciously". The events received enormous publicity. The very name "Peterloo", an ironic echo of the

20 Peterloo: the size of the crowd and the confined space of the square meant that there would inevitably be deaths among the demonstrators once the cavalry were called in.

famous victory at Waterloo in 1815, was a press creation. On 19 August 1819, *The Times* published an influential article blaming the troops. Numerous cartoons soon appeared, showing fat drunken soldiers hacking down defenceless women and children. The radical paper *The Cap of Liberty* accused the Government of "High Treason against the People", calling on the people to arm themselves in self defence. But the most important consequence of Peterloo was that it broadened support for the issue of parliamentary reform; it convinced many, especially from the middle classes, that some change was needed.

The Bristol Riots

Mass demonstrations in favour of reform continued throughout the 1820s, but the worst

◄ 21 Peterloo: the military charged the crowds in St Peter's Square, Manchester during a radical demonstration, and people in the crowd were cut down or trampled underfoot by the cavalry.

violence occurred in 1831, after a Reform Bill introduced by the Whigs in the House of Commons was rejected by the Lords. A National Political Union was formed to provide backing for the Bill, but in Bristol more violent methods were used. Riots broke out on 29 October 1831 on the return to the City of Sir Charles Wetherell, the Recorder of the City, who was a strenuous opponent of the Bill. An observer left the following account:

The riots began on Saturday, continued the whole of Sunday and were only got under control on Monday morning when the corporation, the military, and the citizens awoke from the stupor into which they *appear to have been thrown by this unexpected outbreak of popular fury. The whole of Bristol was now on the verge of destruction; the mansion-house, custom-house, excise office and bishop's palace, were plundered and set on fire; the toll gates pulled down; the prisons burst open with sledge hammers, and their inmates, criminals and debtors, set at liberty amidst the exulting cries of the populace. During the whole of Sunday the mob were the unrestricted masters of the city. Forty two offices, dwelling houses and warehouses were completely destroyed, exclusive of public buildings. The loss of property was estimated at half a million (pounds) . . . .*

Dawson and Wall,
Parliamentary Representation,
Society and Industry in the
Nineteenth Century

22 Sir Charles Wetherell, Recorder of the City of Bristol, had voted against the Reform Bill in Parliament in 1831, and on his return to Bristol he was attacked by a crowd who supported reform.
▼

Rural Discontent: The Swing Riots

23 The attack on Sir Charles Wetherell turned out to be the start of a full-scale riot in Bristol which lasted for days, and did widespread damage to property.

The Bristol riots were only one – though the most destructive – of many popular expressions of support for reform in 1831 and 1832. These same years also saw widespread agricultural discontent. In fact, the years 1830-32 were probably the highest point of social tension in the hundred years from 1750 to 1850. Some radicals such as Gibbon Wakefield believed that the agitation in the countryside was political, influenced by the revolution in France in July 1830. The labouring poor "identified themselves with the heroes of the barricades", the news of whose exploits inflamed them "against those whom they most justly consider as their oppressors". In fact, agricultural rioting was caused by low pay, dislike of tithes and perhaps, above all, opposition to the new threshing machine.

By mid-November 1830 much of the South East of England was affected by machine-breaking and arson. Impending visits by rioters were announced through letters signed by "Captain Swing" (the mythical leader of the riots) so the disturbances are known as the "Swing riots". Groups of labourers would visit a farm to negotiate on wages and the destruction of machines. A typical wage demand was for "2s 6d per day in the summer and 2s in the winter as their wages for work and constant employment".

There was little violence if farmers were sympathetic, but some landowners were roughly treated. In one incident, the rioters brought out a rope, offering the farmers the option of accepting new contracts on wages or the rope. Where farmers refused to break the threshing machines, the rioters did it for them, charging anything between 5s and 40s for their trouble. A troublesome farmer might also have his hayricks burnt. *The Gentleman's Magazine* wrote of a special device used to fire hayricks:

The fire instrument, it appears, is of a slowly explosive character, and being deposited beneath the stack after a certain period ignites and explodes.

The Swing riots broke out sporadically in most parts of England over the years 1830-32. They were especially concentrated, however, in the South East. Agricultural conditions were worst in this area, since there were few

24 "Swing the Rick-burner". Evicted from his farm and cottage for non-payment of tithe, he is explaining his plight to a clergyman. The clergyman is depicted as fat and prosperous compared to the bedraggled labourer and his family.

25 In 1848 the Chartists presented the third, and final petition to parliament. Though the government feared violence, even revolution, the protest collapsed rather ignominiously.

expanding towns to absorb the excess population. Consequently, unemployment was high, and wages low, compared with the Midlands and the North. The government was particularly alarmed at the rapid spread of the Swing riots, coinciding as they did with riots supporting the Reform Movement. Its response was to take a particularly harsh line. Nine rioters were hanged, while no fewer than 464 were transported, which "was the largest batch of prisoners ever transported from England for a common crime".

The Swing disturbances were different from the food riots of the eighteenth century. There was no attempt to control the price of food or to distribute it. Wages and the threat posed by new machinery were at the heart of the dispute, and in this the riots resembled the industrial disputes of the early nineteenth century, such as the activities of the Luddites. The Swing riots were more violent than the food riots of the eighteenth century. The increase in class tensions, which affected the contryside as well as the towns in the early nineteenth century, was evident in the greater degree of violence inflicted on the landowners. Though there was little suggestion of revolution, as there had been at certain times between the 1790s and the 1820s, the years

26 Newport rising, 1839. A group of Chartists, led by John Frost, an ex-magistrate dismissed from his bench for his Chartist activities, attacked Newport. But 28 soldiers, organized by the authorities, easily overpowered them.

between 1830 and 1832 saw more widespread rioting in both town and country than any other two years of the nineteenth, or perhaps any other, century.

Chartist Disturbances

There was little respite from violent protest for the rest of the 1830s. By 1837, opposition to the New Poor Law of 1834 was incorporated into the new working-class protest movement of Chartism. The trade depression of the late 1830s was a major cause of Chartism. By 1842, a combination of a serious trade deficit and high prices produced some of the most serious social conditions of the century. One factory inspector, commenting on unemployment and wage cuts, thought that many workers had either to choose "employment on any terms or starvation". The violence that erupted in 1842

was known as the "Plug riots", since strikers went from pit to pit enforcing further strikes by drawing the plugs from pit engines to make the mines unworkable.

The disturbances began as strikes in the Staffordshire mines over low wages and the truck system in July 1842. By mid-August the strikes were at their height, with large armies of miners moving from town to town, with accompanying violence. At Hanly in the Potteries district of Staffordshire on 14 August, the rioters expressed their support for the Charter, declaring that "all labour would cease until the People's Charter becomes the law of the land". There then followed two days of rioting in which two police stations, one at Hanly, the other at Stoke, were demolished, houses burnt and shops plundered. Troops eventually restored some order to the Potteries, after which 276 people were tried for rioting, five of whom were transported.

Though the Plug riots were centred on the Potteries, they eventually covered a wider area than the Luddite disturbances, spreading to Lancashire, Cheshire, West Riding, Leicestershire and Nottinghamshire. One of the most vivid accounts of the rioters comes from Yorkshire, where 25,000 men were on the move from Todmorden and Bradford towards Halifax.

The sight is just one of those which it is impossible to forget. They came pouring down the wide road in thousands, taking up its whole breadth – a gaunt, famished-looking desperate multitude armed with huge bludgeons, flails, pitchforks and pikes, many without coats and hats and hundred upon hundred with their clothes in rags and tatters. Many of the older men looked sore and weary, but the great bulk of men were in the prime of life, full of wild excitement.

F. Peak, The Risings of the Luddites, Chartists and Plug Drawers, 1895

The Plug riots, like the Luddite outburst, arose out of industrial disputes. Machines such as pit engines were targets for the strikers, but only as a means of ensuring a "turnout" of the workers in that pit. Machines were not the targets of hatred as in the Luddite and Swing riots. In many ways, the 1842 riots were transitional. In their close links with Chartism and attempts to promote a general strike, they looked forward to the more organized industrial and political protest of the later nineteenth century. However, the degree of violence and looting places them in the pattern of early nineteenth-century riots.

Many historians have argued that the period from the 1790s to the 1850s was the most riotous in British history. Industrialization meant the great breakup of traditional communities, the emergence of a new class system and an economy liable to violent fluctuations. Many eighteenth-century riots had enjoyed some support in the wider community, which in turn had restrained their action. The new conditions of the nineteenth century greatly weakened such restraints and changed the nature of riots. Even in the countryside, "wage riots" replaced the traditional food riots. The emergence of a national police force and a powerful trades union movement would eventually reduce the level of violent protest, but in 1850 neither was, as yet, significant.

27 Salter Hebble, Halifax, 1842. The town was the scene of considerable rioting, with clashes between the rioters and the military as can be seen in the picture. 12-15,000 people had marched to the mill of Messrs. John Ackroyd and Son to persuade their workers to join the Chartist strike.
▼

4
A More Orderly Society, 1848-1900

There was a marked decline in the number of riots in the decades after 1848. The late 1830s and 1840s – the era of Chartism and associated riots – mark a peak in the nineteenth century. Thereafter, there was a sharp reduction in disturbances as the following statistics suggest:

Riotous offences per 10,000 population, selected counties:

	1834-48	1849-58	1859-68
Lancashire	7.5	1.9	0.6
Yorkshire	4.1	0.9	1.1
Staffordshire	10.2	1.8	1.0
Cheshire	8.2	1.6	2.3
Warwickshire	3.3	0.8	2.1

Some counties did rise again in the 1860s, but the contrast between the 1840s and later decades is still very marked. The Victorians themselves believed that society was more orderly; a writer commented in the 1870s that:

It may with little fear of contradiction be asserted that there never was, in any nation of which we have a history, a time in which life and property were so secure as they are at present in England.
J. Stevenson, Popular Disturbances in England 1700-1870 *(1979)*

The Police

Popular disturbances continued on a number of issues, especially religious and racial conflicts, at election times, in labour disputes and during political demonstrations in London. Nevertheless, we need to explain the move to a more orderly society. A major factor was the emergence of a police force, eventually on a national scale. Before the development of the police, riot control was in the hands of local magistrates and constables, backed up by the militia or professional troops. As we have seen,

28 The last of the Peelers: Sir Robert Peel founded ➤ his "Peelers" or police constables in London in 1829, and gradually other local authorities followed this example.

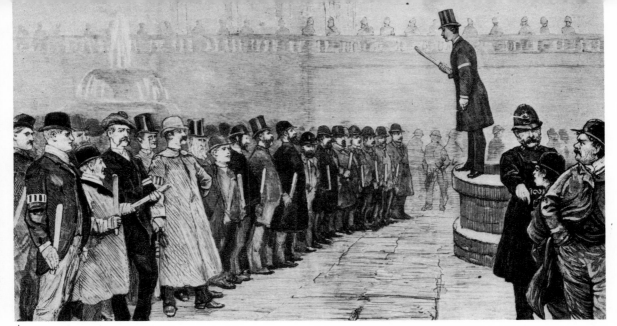

some loss of life in riots was often caused by the
use of troops, which could reflect badly on the
authorities as in the "Peterloo" massacre of
1819.

London received a small group of
professional constables and stipendiary
magistrates in 1792. These proved useful, but
the frequency and scale of riot in early
nineteenth-century London led to demands for
further improvements. In 1829, Robert Peel
established a full-scale Metropolitan Police
Force. This move had been widely resisted. In
1822 a Special Commission set up by Peel had
rejected such a proposal on the grounds that an
effective police force would be irreconcilable
with "that perfect freedom of action and
exemption from interference which are the
great privileges and blessings of society in this
country".

The great advantage of the police over the
military was that they carried truncheons
rather than guns or cutlasses, so they could
disperse a crowd with less threat to life.
Nevertheless, the police were far from popular
in their early days. One constable was killed

and two others stabbed in a riot in London in
1833. However in the 1830s, London "bobbies"
began to show that they could control rioting
without military aid. The Metropolitan force
soon became the most efficient law
enforcement organization in the country.

Initially, the new police were restricted to
London. In 1835 the Municipal Corporations
Act required all boroughs to establish a form of
police system administered by a Watch
Committee and to be paid for out of the local
rates. The standard of borough policing was
not high at first, especially as some boroughs
used their paupers as constables, to save
funds. The 1839 County Police Act permitted
but did not compel counties to establish police
forces. The counties were slow to respond; by
1853 only 22 counties had a force. The Select
Committee on the Police of 1853 ack-
nowledged the 1835 Act as a failure, so in 1856
the County and Borough Police Force Act
made it compulsory for all areas to have their
own police force. Recruitment, however, was
still a problem. There were 1,830 vacancies in
1866 and Lord Woodhouse thought that "the
force was melting away". But the popularity of
the police force as an occupation gradually
increased so that by 1890 there were no
vacancies reported.

The military could still be used for

suppressing riots, but increasingly in the second half of the nineteenth century the government was very reluctant to authorize the use of troops. By the 1890s this advice to local magistrates was typical:

The most important principle is that the calling out of the military to aid in the suppression of rioting should never be resorted to except as a last expedient when there is serious ground for believing that the resources of the civil power will be insufficient; and on this account every possible arrangement should be made beforehand to enable civil authorities to cope with rioters by means of constabulary alone.
D. Richter, Riotous Victorians

Arrangements included borrowing police from neighbouring forces. Also such planning was now easier because riots were less likely to flare up spontaneously and suddenly, and more likely to result from a political demonstration or industrial disputes for which prior warning would be given.

30 During a nine-week weavers' strike in Lancashire in 1878 the house of the employers' leader in Blackburn was looted and burnt down.
▼

Working-Class Organizations

Other factors also led to greater orderliness and a reduction in the incidence of riots. By the end of the 1860s a number of the skilled workers had joined unions, while many had received the vote in 1867. With greater working-class organization, there was much more emphasis on respectability and non-violence. Trade union leaders were well aware that violence could be turned against them in the courts and in the press. In a coal strike in 1871, when miners were faced with eviction from their "tied" cottages by the coal owners, the union leaders issued the following advice:

Stay in the house, your families around, lock the door (as against an ordinary house-breaker) sit down or go to bed, firmly and quietly state that you have read in a book that "an Englishman's home is his castle". Beyond that, offer no resistance whatsoever. Let them carry you out.

As more workers received the vote, and the franchise was further extended in 1884, trades union and working-class organizations tried to improve conditions by putting pressure on the political parties. There was less need to resort to riot.

When all these points have been made, however, there were still numerous riots in Victorian England. Some disturbances resulted from trades union activity, which was not always as peaceful as its leaders wanted. In a nine-week weavers' strike in north east Lancashire in 1878, for example, the house of the employers' association leader was looted and burned. Troops had to be called in to a strike at Hall Colliery near Featherstone in September 1893. They were greeted with volleys of stones and when the troops opened fire, two people were killed. Nevertheless, Dr J. Stevenson, in his important book *Popular Disturbances in England 1700-1870* has concluded that:

Although strikes were to appear a major cause of popular disturbances after 1870 they in fact reflected the increasing emphasis on order and restraint in the conduct of industrial disputes.

Election Disturbances

Elections continued to be an important source of disturbance. This was the case throughout the nineteenth century. Cobbett described how his opponents had hired a mob to attack his supporters at the Coventry election of 1820:

The Ruffians came, not less than five hundred in number, in regular order, about eight or ten deep, with drums and banners at their head. They made their approach by the higher part and the ground, and began the attack on my voters. All attempts to resist were in vain. And in five minutes, three hundred of my voters were as completely driven as if an army had made an attack on them. After this not a man dared to show his face to vote for me.

Reitzel (ed.), Autobiography of William Cobbett

The 1868 election was one of the more important ones in the century. There was an

▲
31 In 1867 most urban workers had received the vote, but rural labourers were still unfranchised. Here we see a demonstration in favour of further parliamentary reform.

enlarged electorate after the Reform Act of 1867, while significant political issues, such as the disestablishment of the Irish Church and the problems of Ireland in general, were widely debated. Both anti-Irish and anti-Catholic feeling were already high in Lancashire, and a municipal election in Blackburn provided the worst scenes. The Tories, it seemed, had taken the initiative. The *Annual Register* reported:

A cart of stones was kept in readiness by the blue and orange [Tory] party, and a crowd of women kept supplying them with missiles. Most of the rioters were armed with picking stones about two feet high in length and one to one and a half inches thick at the head. All along the pavement streams of blood were flowing, and the sickening sight of men with blood flowing from their heads and faces met one at every turn. The police charged the mob with drawn cutlasses and truncheons, committing great havoc, but they did not succeed in restoring even comparative calm for a long time.

Blackburn schools had to be turned into hospitals to accommodate the injured. The use of cutlasses by the police is significant. Such a use would have been unlikely later in the century.

Changes in the electoral system such as the Secret Ballot Act of 1872 and the Corrupt Practices Act of 1883 helped to make elections more orderly. In London it was said that the Ballot Act had transformed the situation so that "the places that used to be the worst are now the best". Also, disturbances were now more likely to occur during the campaign rather than during the poll itself. But violence at elections did not disappear quickly. In the 1885 election many mobs were reported intimidating voters. The Suffolk police were occupied for days controlling electoral disturbances. *The Times* remarked succinctly "Never was there such a hurly burly." One reason why elections were still likely to lead to disturbances was that for many of the population they remained a major form of amusement and an excuse for heavy drinking, in an era deficient in public amusements.

Anti-Catholic (Anti-Irish) Riots

The increased use of Irish labour as railway navvies in the 1830s and 1840s contributed to a revival of anti-Catholicism in mid-Victorian Britain. The activities of the Fenians – a terrorist group demanding independence for Ireland – in the 1860s further heightened anti-Irish feeling. Even respectable publications such as *The Times* showed anti-Catholicism in an editorial of 1853:

We very much doubt whether in England or indeed in any free Protestant country, a true Papist can be a good subject.

Counties such as Lancashire had the highest religious and racial tensions.

32 Fenians attack a van in Manchester, 1867.
▼

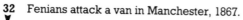

▲
33 The Birmingham "No Popery" riots. Religious riots were among the most violent in the nineteenth century, and anti-Catholic demonstrations were often closely linked to anti-Irish feeling.

Lancashire had possessed a strong Catholic minority since the sixteenth century, while the North West was the area of highest Irish immigration. Many towns in the North West had their Irish quarters or "Little Ireland" as they were known. This part of the country was therefore fertile territory for Protestant rabble rousers such as William Murphy. An ex-Catholic, Murphy was sponsored by the Protestant Evangelical Mission to preach on the theme of "No Popery". Murphy's language was of the most inflammatory kind, saying that "the priests of Rome were murderers, cannibals, pickpockets and liars".

In 1868, William Murphy announced his intention of touring Lancashire, including the cotton town of Ashton.

I am going to Ashton to lecture in the cotton mill, and within 300 to 400 yards of the

Catholic Chapel, and it will not take long to drive the Popish lambs to Paddy's land. If the people once break out in Lancashire, they will seize first the Catholic priests, then the Sisters of Mercy, and afterwards the lambs [i.e. ordinary Catholics] and send them all afloat neck and crop.

D. Richter, Riotous Victorians

Murphy did not restrict his anti-Catholicism to words alone. After his lecture he encouraged Protestants to assemble in Reynor Row, Ashton at 7 p.m. on 12 May 1868.

41

Their target was the poor Irish Catholic quarter of Reynor Row.

The rioters met with little or no opposition and in a very short time every house in the row was forcibly entered, the window frames and doors smashed to atoms and the furniture and bedding were hurled into the streets where they were burnt. Tables, chairs, sofas, pictures, ornaments and carpets – all were thrown into one heterogeneous mass and consumed by flames.

D. Richter, Riotous Victorians

Murphy, who had lived by violence, died by it. On Sunday, 20 April 1871, he was about to

34   The authorities were impressed by the sober behaviour of the crowds celebrating Queen Victoria's Diamond Jubilee, and this is often seen as evidence that English society was more "orderly" by the end of the nineteenth century.
▼

give a lecture at the Oddfellows Hall, Whitehaven. A group of Irish Catholic labourers from Cleator Moor, a small mining town just down the coast from Whitehaven, arrived early. They seized Murphy, threw him down a flight of stairs and kicked him, until he was rescued by the police. Though he lived for another year, he eventually died from the injuries he had received that night.

"Anti-Popery" should not be seen just as a mark of Victorian religious feeling. Catholics and Irish were easy scapegoats for other ills, and the "anti-Popery" cry was a traditional excuse for disturbance. In fact, Protestant organizations such as the Salvation Army, especially in their early days, also provoked rowdy opposition. One elderly citizen of Worthing in Sussex in 1884, objected to their "beating tambourines to the great annoyance of peaceful inhabitants". In August 1885, when contingents from various branches of the Salvation Army met at Derby, they were followed by 6,000-7,000 "anti-Salvationists". Vicious hand-to-hand fighting followed in the market place at Derby. The anti-Salvationists then attacked the Salvation Army barracks, smashing windows and band instruments. The following evening, the "antis" celebrated their victory by overturning crates of rotten peas in the market place and hurling them in all directions.

Nevertheless, by the 1870s, the middle-class values of orderliness and sobriety were filtering through to the working class, especially to the more skilled workers. Large assemblies and demonstrations were now less likely to get out of hand, as Edward Hamilton, Gladstone's private secretary remarked about Queen Victoria's Golden Jubilee Day Celebrations:

The most remarkable feature of the evening was the extraordinary good nature and orderliness of the crowds on the streets. A few years ago festivity and drunkedness were among the masses almost synonomous terms – we can flatter ourselves that we have recently become more orderly and sober and have made great advances in the art of organisation. Rowdyism and rough horseplay which have usually characterised large English assemblies have been conspicuous by their absence.

Demonstrations in London

One important political issue still led to disturbances: the right to hold political demonstrations in the capital itself. Many of the traditional London meeting areas, such as Spa Fields and St George's Fields, had been covered in buildings by the 1840s. The main open spaces left in central London were Hyde Park and Trafalgar Square. The former was Crown property, as were several other of the major parks, while Trafalgar Square was also vested in the Queen by an Act of 1844, but in practice was controlled by the Home Office. Consequently, the Crown and the Home Office had the power to restrict access to almost all the possible meeting places for a large demonstration in London. Also, the Seditious Meetings Act of 1817 had forbidden meetings of fifty or more people within a mile of Westminster when Parliament was in session.

The use of Hyde Park led to violent clashes in July 1855. Police Commissioner Sir Richard Mayne issued a notice on 29 June, declaring unlawful a proposed meeting against the Sunday Trading Bill on 1 July. This was widely regarded as being of dubious legality. Consequently, on Sunday, 1 July no fewer than 150,000 people assembled in Hyde Park to protest against restrictions on Sunday trading, but also to assert their right of meeting at Hyde Park. The police were jeered at and after suffering a fair amount of provocation, charged the crowd and took seventy-two prisoners. The press took up the issue of police brutality and the government was forced to appoint a Commission Inquiry, whose report was highly critical of police action.

The behaviour of the police was an issue closely connected with the right of demonstration in Hyde Park and Trafalgar

[the police] have always been taught to show the utmost forbearance that be expected of any Englishman.

Square. Demonstrations were organized for propaganda purposes; their aim was peaceful demonstration, to stress the reasonableness of their action, while blaming any violence on the police. By the 1880s the police themselves were aware that they were involved in a propaganda war with the demonstrators. Commissioner Henderson, writing in 1886, noted that the police:

are very much afraid of showing too much zeal because they know perfectly well that the public is quite ready to say if there is a disturbance that they provoked it, and they

All the issues of the right to demonstrate, the effectiveness of police organization and the relative blame attached to the crowd and the police for the ensuing violence were most evident in the Trafalgar Square disturbances of November 1887. Police Commissioner Charles Warren decided to impose a ban on marching in Trafalgar Square on Tuesday, 8 November, fearing a demonstration on the Wednesday of the Lord Mayor's Day. The ban succeeded in that week, but by Sunday, 13 November various radical organizations, including two left-wing groups, the Social Democratic Federation and the Socialist League, were determined to march on Trafalgar Square.

36 The Trafalgar Square riots. Crowds who had gathered to observe the demonstration cheer the parade of the military as the cavalry move into position for the demonstrations.

Police precautions were elaborate. By 10 a.m. on Sunday 13, 1,500 constables had cordoned off the open spaces of Trafalgar Square, standing two deep all around the central part of the square and four deep facing Whitehall. An extra 300 were at Nelson's Column, with 100 cavalry police, armed with revolvers, in front of the Grand Hotel; 2,500 reserve constables were in Charing Cross, 100 at Hyde Park and scores of others in all the main thoroughfares leading to Trafalgar Square. With both the Grenadier and Life Guards held in reserve, the elaborate preparations were sufficient to "repel something short of a popular insurrection" according to John Mackail, the biographer of William Morris.

The two main wings of the demonstration were a crowd of some 8,000 from South London and one of 5,000 from the East End. The South London contingent approached Westminster Bridge singing the "Marseillaise" and "Starving for Old England". The police blocked the bridge, but with arms linked the crowd forced its way across, though twenty-six of their members were taken off to St Thomas's Hospital, just by the bridge. The East London crowd was intercepted by the police in The Strand near Waterloo Place, but in the clash Inspector Livingston suffered a broken nose from a man wielding a stone in a handkerchief. Despite the challenge by the police, most groups, though dispersed, managed to reach Trafalgar Square.

The crowd was not allowed to enjoy Trafalgar Square for long. A battalion of Grenadier Guards marched into the northern part of the Square shouldering rifles with fixed bayonets. Meanwhile the police cavalry, charging with batons, dispersed the crowd in the southern part. Within forty minutes Trafalgar Square was emptying fast; the crowd was on the run. As a result of the demonstrations – or "Bloody Sunday" as it was subsequently known – two demonstrators died, 200 were taken to hospital, while seventy-seven constables were injured, mainly with broken noses or bitten fingers.

37 Mounted police charge the crowd in the Trafalgar Square demonstrations. The demonstrators blamed the police for the violence on this "Bloody Sunday" but some, including an American visitor, thought the police acted with restraint.

38 Bloody Sunday 1887. The South London contingent in the Trafalgar Square protests march over Westminster Bridge, having broken through a strong police barrier.

The main point at issue over Bloody Sunday was whether the leaders of the demonstration, John Burns, a working-class Scottish engineer and Robert Bentine Cunningham Graham, MP for North West Lanarkshire, were to blame for the violence, or whether the police were. An American visitor who watched the main events from the National Liberal Club, wrote that "the much abused London police showed a spirit of moderation towards the mob which they would not receive in any American city". Graham and Burns, though sent to prison for six months for an unlawful assembly, were acquitted on the more serious charge of causing a riot. Burns protested that, armed only "with a pocket handkerchief and a

tramway ticket", he was ill-equipped to riot. Defence counsel for the two leaders tried to put the blame on the police.

> *It was an ordinary London crowd which, if not interfered with and allowed to go its own way, would behave in a perfectly proper and law abiding manner. Mr Graham and Mr Burns were going unarmed and peacefully to assert what they believed to be the right of meeting in Trafalgar Square, but the police lost their heads, dashed upon them, and provoked a conflict which, but for the misguided action of the police, would not have occurred.*
>
> D. Richter, Riotous Victorians

Late nineteenth-century disturbances such as those in Trafalgar Square on Bloody Sunday mark the arrival of the modern form of political unrest. The purpose of such a demonstration is to establish the right to march and protest, sometimes in defiance of a ban. The objective is to gain maximum publicity for a cause, often by provoking a well-organized police into some kind of violent action, so that the authorities are seen in the poorest light. The modern disturbance is to a great extent a propaganda battle, but still comes under the legal definition of riot.

39 Rioting in the West End. Despite a reduction in rioting in the second half of the nineteenth century, casual incidents of violence, especially in large towns, were still common, and frequently involved looting.

5
Political and Industrial Violence Between the Wars

During the first three months of 1919 unrest touched its high-water mark. I do not think that at any time in history since the Bristol Riots we have been so near revolution . . . . On 27 January there were extensive strikes on the Clyde of a revolutionary rather than an economic character.

This was the opinion of Sir Basil Thomson, Head of Special Branch, writing in 1922. Looking back on the events of 1919 some years later, William Gallacher, then a leading shop steward, thought that "a rising was expected. A rising should have taken place. The workers were ready and able to effect it; the leadership had never thought of it".

The Fear of Revolution

The fear that disturbances would lead not to the traditional clash with authorities but to revolution, was common immediately after World War One. The successful Communist revolution in Russia in 1917 had inspired other risings elsewhere in Europe. In Britain itself there had been a growth of left-wing ideas such as Syndicalism and the emergence of a small Communist Party. Now, the fears of revolution appear to have been largely unfounded. The serious industrial unrest of the 1920s and the politically inspired hunger marches of the 1930s both led to violent disturbances, but it is significant that between

1919 and 1974 there was not a single death from riot in England. Both anti-Catholic and election riots declined sharply, and, in many respects, this period saw a continuation of a more orderly society.

The disturbances which led Sir Basil Thomson to think that Britain was near revolution started on Clydeside in January 1919. The strike was over a forty-hour week, and on the first day 40,000 men came out. Soon the numbers were 70,000 and on 29 January a delegation of strikers met the Lord Provost of Glasgow to explain their case. The strikers alarmed the Provost sufficiently for him to send a telegram to the Cabinet in London. He

40 Labour unrest, Glasgow 1919. The action of the police in Glasgow in 1919 was considered provocative even by sympathetic sources such as the *Glasgow Herald.*
▼

A STRIKER STRUCK : AN INCIDENT IN ONE OF THE BATON CHARGES BY THE POLICE.

asked the Cabinet to consider the situation urgently, since the strikers had "hitherto adopted constitutional methods" but threatened that "they would adopt any other methods which they might consider would be likely to advance their cause".

The Liberal Cabinet needed little convincing of the possibility of revolution. Early in 1919 revolution seemed to be looming in many parts of Europe, and the Sparticist revolt in Berlin had just been suppressed. The Prime Minister Bonar Law thought that "if the movement in Glasgow grew, it would spread all over the country". All of the Cabinet, with the exception of Churchill, agreed to the use of troops if necessary. A senior Scottish Office official was sent to Glasgow to liaise between the Provost and the government in London.

Violence broke out in Glasgow on Friday, 31 January, but led by the police rather than by revolutionary strikers. Crowds of strikers had gathered in St George's Square, Glasgow, to hear Bonar Law's reply to the Provost's telegram. The *Glasgow Herald*, a paper generally hostile to the strikers, gave a vivid account of police action as they proceeded to clear St George's Square.

With a vigour and determination that was a prelude to extraordinary scenes . . . and to which the city, with all its acquaintance with labour troubles, could happily offer no parallel. A strong body of police swept the crowd in front of them, raining a hurricane of blows which fell indiscriminately on those actually participating in the strike and those who had been drawn to the scene mainly by curiosity.

The Cabinet, not surprisingly, received a different version of events. The Minister of Labour reported on the same Friday afternoon that "he had no details but understood that foot and mounted police had charged the crowd in order to quell a riot, and casualties had resulted". Immediately, troops were moved to Glasgow – in fact, 12,000 troops, 100 lorries and six tanks. By Monday, 2 February six tanks were in place in the cattle market in the East End of Glasgow.

However, far from signalling a revolution, "Bloody Friday", 31 January, was the high point of the strike. Within two weeks the strike was over, as the effects of the loss of wages hit hard. Two of the main leaders, Emmanuel Shinwell, later a distinguished Labour MP and peer, and William Gallacher, later a member of the Communist Party, were given five and three months respectively, for incitement to riot and rioting. The Lord Advocate prosecuting for the Crown declared that "the incidents on January 31 in George Square constituted the gravest imaginable menace to public order and security". In fact, the strike was probably rather a weak affair. Except for the Scottish T.U.C., there was little official union backing, and there was no serious attempt to spread the action outside Glasgow. Left to itself, the strike would probably have collapsed without violence. It was the police and the tanks that gave a dramatic quality to an otherwise run-of-the-mill industrial dispute.

41 Once violence had erupted between police and strikers, the strikers retired behind barricades, but were still subjected to repeated baton charges by the police.

▼

BARRICADED : POLICE RETURNING FROM A BATON CHARGE IN NORTH FREDERICK STREET, WHERE MISSILES WERE THROWN.

▲
42 Demonstrations in London were used increasingly between the wars as a means of publicizing a particular cause. Here, 20,000 Civil Servants protest against salary cuts imposed because of the economic crisis of 1931. Such demonstrations were generally peaceful.

Unemployment Demonstrations

Although industrial relations remained bitter in the 1920s, culminating in the General Strike of 1926, the level of public violence was relatively low. With mounting unemployment in the 1930s, however, there was an increase in public demonstrations, some of which involved riot. The National Unemployed Workers' Movement, or N.U.W.M., was the most important organization of the unemployed during the Depression. It had been founded in 1921 as a militant organization to campaign on behalf of the unemployed. From the beginning, it had close connections with the Communist Party of Great Britain. Its most important leader, Walter Hannington, a shop steward from London, was also a founder member of the Communist Party. In 1929 the N.U.W.M. had

about 10,000 members, but by the end of 1931, this figure had reached 37,000. In October 1931 the N.U.W.M. had been responsible for organizing the major demonstrations on which 100 arrests had been made.

The worst violence occurred in September 1932 at Birkenhead. Trouble had been simmering throughout August and early September. A demonstration of 3,000 unemployed had taken place on 7 September, with the N.U.W.M. putting forward a radical programme of an end to the means test, the extension of work schemes, increased unemployment relief and a 25% reduction in council house rents. The Mayor refused to see the demonstrators, but agreed to call a special council meeting for Tuesday, 15 September. A crowd waited for five hours to hear the Council's views. When only vague promises were offered, the police had to use baton charges to disperse the crowd. Discontent continued throughout Wednesday, 16 September, but it was on Thursday that the town erupted.

Events were sparked off by a Communist-organized march to the Birkenhead Public Assistance Committee's Office to demand directly increased unemployment relief. The

49

43 Protests over unemployment were often less peaceful than demonstrations by respectable groups such as the Civil Servants, and the Government feared social unrest in 1920. Large numbers of police were used to control this rally by the unemployed in Whitehall in 1920.

P.A.C. tried to stall the crowd, which then, under its own momentum, went to the house of Alderman Baker, Chairman of the P.A.C. The police arrived as the crowd was pelting the house with stones. A local newspaper reported that "Batons were wielded to good effect by the police, who scattered flying ranks of the mob in all directions, leaving about fifty of them lying screaming and shouting in the road". But this was only the beginning of the riot. In the northern part of the town, the "Co-Op" store was smashed and looted. Iron railings were torn up in the park and used as weapons against the police. The battle went on for several hours, with thirty-seven demonstrators and seven policemen treated in hospital.

Violence erupted again on the Friday evening, after the police had broken up a political meeting. They tried to follow the crowds into the narrow streets that surrounded the docks, where they met a kind of guerilla resistance among a maze of alleys and courtyards. Rioting occurred again on Saturday, 19 September. Sixteen shops were broken into and looted, and there was a pitched battle between 400 rioters, armed with iron railings and bottles, and the police. Women joined in by throwing furniture from upstairs windows at the police. The Liverpool police were ferried across the Mersey in the early hours of Sunday morning to reinforce the local Birkenhead force. Three days later there were disturbances in Liverpool itself and further violence also took place in places as far apart as West Ham, London and North Shields.

There was a massive demonstration in London by the unemployed in late October 1932. Contingents arrived from all over the country, and at least 15-20,000 were expected to demonstrate outside the House of Commons to present a petition. *The Daily Telegraph* saw only the hand of Wal Hannington and the Communists in the London hunger riots.

> *How long is London to be subjected to the indignity of having its police forces – regular and special – mobilised to deal with the Communist HANNINGTON and his Marchers, but in reality with HANNINGTON and the revolutionary riff-raff of London? Ninety per cent of the Marchers may well be dupes, pawns in a Communist game directed by the master-intriguers of Moscow . . . . The abolition of the Means Test is a pretext. The presentation of a Petition is a blind.*

Although there were many thousand demonstrators who clashed frequently with the police, the arrest of Wal Hannington and the seizure of the mass petition from the cloakroom at Charing Cross Railway Station by the police led to the collapse of the demonstration. Contingents of demonstrators from various parts of the country were escorted to their respective railway stations by the police on 5 November 1932, and this marked the end of the demonstration in the capital.

1932 was the worst year for riots. Police action in 1931-32 had been tough; in June 1932 in Bristol riots were caused by the ruthlessness of the police. The *Bristol Evening Post* said that there was "no hint of trouble" in a N.U.W.M. demonstration until:

> *suddenly there emerged from side streets and shop doorways a strong body of police*

> *reinforcements with batons drawn. They set about clearing the streets. Men fell left and right under their charge . . . . The cries of men and the terrified shrieking of women added to the tumult. Then came a troop of mounted police charging through Castle Street from the Old Market Street end, scattering the last of the demonstrators. In a few minutes the streets were clear, save for the men who lay with cracked heads, groaning on the pavements and in shop doorways, where they had staggered for refuge.*

The government endorsed the police's tough policy. Along with many others, the government was alarmed by what it saw as a Communist-inspired attempt to bring disorder to British streets. But there was also another point at issue. Both the N.U.W.M. and the government were trying to win over public opinion, to win the propaganda battle. The government could generally rely on the conservative press to support its hard line against the marchers, and news cameras were not allowed to film some demonstrations, such as the one in London in October 1932.

By 1934, when another wave of hunger marches was being planned, the situation had changed. Government and police action was scrutinized far more closely after the formation of the national Council for Civil Liberties in 1934. The Council included several prominent figures such as Clement Attlee, Edith Summerskill, Harold Laski, Kingsley Martin and H.G. Wells. In a letter sent to the *Manchester Guardian* just before another N.U.W.M. march, they said they intended "to maintain vigilant observation of the proceedings of the next few days". They argued that the atmosphere of alarm created by the government seemed in their view "unjustified by the facts".

By 1936 the N.U.W.M. itself was far more moderate, and the main purpose of its activity seemed to be to win over public opinion rather than to mobilize mass support. In this different climate, the government also adopted

▲
44 The Jarrow Marchers in London, 1936. Though there were many such "hunger marches" in the 1930s, the media gave especially sympathetic treatment to the Jarrow March because, unlike many others, it was not organized by the left wing NUWM.

somewhat different tactics. Firstly they tried to discredit the N.C.C.L., which had frequently given evidence on police misbehaviour in demonstrations. The Home Office described the Council as having "close subterranean connections with the Communist Party". The press and media also responded by treating N.U.W.M. marches differently from others. The Jarrow March, which was not organized by the N.U.W.M., was given sympathetic and widespread coverage by the media. *The Times*, for example, ran a full-column report, in which it praised the endurance of the marchers and brought in the human element with stories of the marchers' blistered feet. A much larger N.U.W.M. march arrived in London a week after the Jarrow March, but was virtually ignored by the press.

Although the government took a hard line in the early 1930s, and tried to exploit public alarm, the demonstrations organized by the N.U.W.M. were often likely to lead to riot, even if their intentions fell short of revolution. Their language was inflammatory, encouraging "mass struggle on the streets", "mass and stormy activity against the authorities" and "day to day mass rallies, steadily mounting in force and intensity". But compared to the nineteenth-century disturbances or urban riots of the eighteenth century, the extent of violence was very restricted. Except in the Merseyside riots, damage to property was limited and the only loss of life was suffered by two demonstrators in Belfast in 1932. Also, in almost all the disturbances, casualties among the demonstrators far outnumbered those among the police. In the London disturbances of October 1932, for example, sixty-eight demonstrators were injured compared to only nine policemen.

Fascism in the 1930s

The British Union of Fascists provoked public disturbances from the end of 1933, though few were directly involved in riots. But the violence shown by the Fascists led to retaliation which sometimes ended in riotous disturbances. Trouble began in 1933, with Fascists selling their newspapers in the East End of London. Fascist newspapers contained strongly anti-Jewish material, while the East End contained a high proportion of Jews. A typical incident occurred on 7 May 1933, when a group of Jews attacked a man selling Fascist newspapers. Eight Jews were arrested, a crowd assembled to protest, and police dispersed them.

45 Blackshirts in London, 1933. The Blackshirts were a common sight in London streets from late 1932, and in February 1933 the British Fascist Party launched its own newspaper *The Blackshirt*, being distributed here by party workers.

A meeting of the British Union of Fascists at Olympia on 7 June 1934 threatened public order much more. There were 12,000 present, 2,000 of them uniformed Blackshirts. Also there were a large number of anti-Fascist demonstrators both inside and outside the Hall. The police had only 742 men on duty, "barely sufficient to prevent a serious disturbance starting, which might have finished in disorder, injuries and very serious damage to property". In fact, any real threat of riot was checked by the action of the Fascist stewards who policed the meeting themselves, but in a violent manner. Hecklers were ejected from the meeting, as police evidence noted later:

> At intervals the door was flung open and one or more persons ejected into the main road. In nearly every case they were bleeding from the head and the face and their clothing was badly torn . . . the situation was at periods a little ugly, but in almost all these cases it was through the action of the stewards.

Disturbances caused by clashes between Fascists and anti-Fascists continued and

reached a climax in 1936. There were disorders involving the British Union of Fascists at the Carfax Assembly Room at Oxford on 25 May, at Hulme, Manchester on 28 June, at Hull on 12 July, at Bristol in August and at Leeds on 27 September. The worst disturbances, however, occurred from clashes between Fascists and anti-Fascists in the Battle of Cable Street, on Sunday, 4 October 1936. This was the final straw for the government, which decided to pass the Public Order Act. This Act, which became law on 1 January 1937, made the wearing of uniforms for political purposes in a public place, an offence. It also made it an offence to organize meetings "for the use or display of physical force in promoting any political objective".

Despite the new Public Order Act, disturbances continued, as the East End police made clear in April 1937:

The marchers are often carried away by their anti-Jewish feeling, and acts of damage occur. The unfortunate inhabitants are deprived of sleep, and some of them are more or less terror stricken, for the Jewish resident of the East End, the Fascist is a source of grave apprehension. The activity is not all one sided, as the Jewish and Communist elements too are active, and their meetings and processions need quite as much policing. It is quite plain that offence breeds reprisal and the parties are being forced wider apart.

Fascist activity in the East End continued at a high level, and in November-December 1938 there were some 103 small meetings. Throughout 1939 the Metropolitan Police recorded Fascist meetings making provocative anti-Jewish remarks. Though they were not a major cause of riot in the 1930s, the British Union of Fascists contributed to an ugly undercurrent of public violence from 1933 onwards.

46 Though Mosley, leader of the British Fascists, always claimed that the Blackshirts rejected violence, he stressed equally that they would meet "force by force" and clashes between Fascists and left-wing groups were frequent.

▼

Conclusion

In the absence of comparable statistics, it is difficult to judge disturbances between the wars against nineteenth-century riots. There were some very violent disturbances, as in Merseyside in 1932, which involved considerable loss of property. Nevertheless, the eighteenth and nineteenth-century practice of burning property had ceased, and only in Belfast was there any loss of life when two rioters were killed in 1932. Moreover, protests against mass unemployment in the 1930s became less violent with time, as both the N.U.W.M. and the police tried to win over public opinion by being more restrained and disciplined. Though fears of revolution were revived in the early 1930s with rising unemployment, political reality was quite different. For many of the unemployed, a form of fatalism was the overriding reaction. The reaction George Orwell found in Wigan may have been widespread: people there "neither turned revolutionary nor lost their self-respect; merely they kept their tempers and settled down to make the best of things on a fish and chip standard".

47 On formal occasions such as this May Day parade of 1938 the Fascists put on their most respectable front to project themselves as a well ordered and disciplined party.
▼

6
From Order to Riots
1950-1980s

In 1981 Britain was shocked by a wave of urban riots. Both in Britain and abroad people were taken aback; it seemed to be so out of character. In fact, we have described a history of violent protest over the last three centuries in Britain. But in more recent times Britain has acquired a reputation as a peaceful society. George Orwell had written in his *Inside the Whale and Other Essays* that "gentleness and respect for the law were two outstanding qualities of the English". The 1940s and late 1950s seemed to endorse Orwell's view. From the late 1960s, however, some increasingly violent protest was evident, though the riots of 1981 were different from anything preceding them.

Public violence occurred in the 1950s, despite the general air of civil peace. The most significant of these outbreaks were the race riots of 1958 in the Notting Hill district of London. In retrospect these seem limited and appear to have left little permanent mark. The 1950s also saw the emergence of ritualized violence between teenage gangs such as "Mods" and "Rockers". Each would descend on the same seaside resort during the Easter and

◄ **48** Little public violence was seen in British streets in the first two decades after World War Two, but this relative tranquillity was broken by ritualistic fighting between rival youth cults of "Mods" and "Rockers".

▲
50 Anti-Vietnam War demonstration. Protests over America's involvement in Vietnam, and the general mood of radicalism among the young middle classes, especially university students, brought about a great increase in the number of political demonstrations by the late 1960s.

▲
49 Over the last two decades there has been a steady increase in violence among rival football fans and this scene has become a familiar one.

Whitsun weekend holidays to fight one another and the police.

Another form of public violence that emerged in the 1950s and that has continued to grow is that between rival fans at football matches. There appear to be as many theories about the growth in football hooliganism as riots on the football grounds themselves. A number of factors may have played a part. Families move around more today so that children are less likely to feel part of a community. Advertisers in particular have stressed that teenagers are different from the rest of the family. This, together with other general trends, has weakened authority in the family.

The main social and economic developments after World War Two, however, tended towards a more peaceful society. The growth of the welfare state and above all the benefits of full employment and a rising standard of living, removed many of the traditional causes of rioting. By the late 1960s, however, significant changes were taking place. The growth of radical politics, taking as its model the Civil Rights Movement in America, led to a revival of mass demonstrations to publicize political views. In 1968 violence erupted in Ulster which ever since that date has provided images of public violence on the television. The impact of Ulster on the rest of Britain is difficult to gauge, but Northern Ireland has certainly shown other British rioters how to make an improvised petrol bomb. By the 1970s there were outbreaks of industrial violence, seen perhaps most overtly in attacks on building workers by the "Shrewsbury pickets". The issue of "flying pickets" was in some ways new, though they were a feature of the Plug riots of the 1840s.

51 From the later 1960s there has been a continuous level of violence on the streets of Belfast, previously unknown in British history. Scenes like this one have become commonplace on our television screens.

Political Demonstrations

The major cause of disorder in the early 1970s was political demonstrations. In 1972 the first death since 1919 as a result of riot or public disturbance occurred in England. This happened at the Red Lion Square demonstration in June. The Red Lion Square demonstration was only one of 1,321 political protests in London in the years 1972-74, though only 54 of them involved disorder. In these public disturbances of the early 1970s, the majority of demonstrators were students

or recent university graduates. This marks them out as different from earlier examples of protest.

The demonstration that led to the death of Kevin Gately started as a protest march by the London Area Council for Liberation, against a march by the National Front. Both marches planned to converge on Red Lion Square in London, Liberation for an open air meeting, the National Front for a rally inside Conway Hall. The police naturally planned to keep the two sides apart. However, a group within Liberation, the International Marxist Group, charged the police cordon in Red Lion Square to try to picket the entrance to Conway Hall. Scuffles occurred and the demonstrators eventually withdrew. A number of people were left on the ground. One of them was Kevin Gately, who died some hours later.

Liberation supporters immediately blamed the police for Gately's death but all the evidence brought out in the Scarman Report suggests that he was killed either by a glancing blow from a banner pole or trampled upon by the crowd. Lord Justice Scarman put the blame for the violence squarely on the International Marxist Group, whose assault, he said was "a deliberate, determined and sustained attack . . . . It was unexpected, unprovoked and viciously violent". However the police also came in for criticism for their action in leading a baton charge later in the afternoon. The *Guardian* was the most critical of the media, with headlines of "Left Guilty of First Charge – Police of Second."

By the middle of the 1970s, unemployment was rising, as was the crime rate. These, together with the racial issue, gave extremist parties such as the National Front material to exploit. In August 1977 the National Front decided to hold a rally in Deptford and Lewisham. This area was one where the immigration issue was easily exploited, with a coloured population of 14%. The National Front wanted to show the white population "that they were not forgotten". The Socialist Workers' Party (then called the International Socialists) immediately organized a counter-

▲
52 Some of the worst violence in English streets in recent years has come from extreme left-wing groups protesting against the right of the National Front to march. Here police grapple with anti-National Front protestors at Lewisham.

demonstration. The Socialist Workers called on their supporters to "drive the Nazis off the streets" and to "stop the Nazi marching whatever the authorities do".

By the afternoon of Saturday, 13 August, the atmosphere in Lewisham was ugly. The National Front had posters proclaiming that "80% of Muggers are black" while the Socialist Workers' Party had posters with the headline "The Police are the real muggers". A group of Millwall football supporters gathering for the match chanted "up the National Front – kill the blacks." The S.W.P. demonstrators, occupying derelict buildings, threw bottles, dustbins and stones at the N.F. marchers. Once the police intervened, the S.W.P. attacked them. Two policemen were stabbed. Numerous weapons were confiscated including carving knives and a large iron pipe studded with bolts. Altogether, 134 people were injured in the clashes.

There seems little doubt that the S.W.P. was intent on violence on 13 August 1977. Steve Jeffreys, the S.W.P. National Organizer, in an interview with *The Times*, stated:

> *The stone and bottle throwing tactics of demonstrators at Lewisham has been justified and necessary . . . . We want to make it absolutely clear to the police that we are not going to allow the Nazis to walk the streets of this country. We shall do everything to stop them.*

Though the Lewisham riots were politically motivated, the issues they exploited look forward to the spontaneous riots at St Paul's, Bristol, Brixton and Toxteth within the next few years.

Brixton, Toxteth and Others

In the spring and summer of 1981 in many British cities mobs of people, mostly young and black and many unemployed, rioted with considerable violence. Both property and police were attacked. The violence was a shock, but scarcely a surprise. There had been a number of warnings. In Bristol in April 1980 raids on a popular café called the "Black and White", had led to the kind of disorders on a small scale which the riots of 1981 exactly mirrored.

Though the riots involved a high proportion of black youths, only one of the major outbreaks of 1981 could be described as a "race riot". This was the disturbance at Southall in west London where militant white rascists attacked members of the local Asian community. They were driven off by force. Elsewhere clashes were not between black and white – except that many rioters were black and most of the police were white. Violence was generally directed against property and the police rather than against neighbours of other races.

Lord Scarman, in his report on the Brixton

riots of mid-1981, wrote:

The British public watched with horror and incredulity an instant audio-visual presentation on their television sets of scenes of violence and disorder in their capital city the like of which had not previously been seen in this century in Britain.

In fact, violence had first broken out in Brixton in April on the evening of Friday, 10 April. In one weekend, much property was destroyed, and several hundred policemen and several dozen citizens were injured.

The long-established black community had complained for years about police discrimination. A report commissioned by the Lambeth Borough Council in January 1981 described the harassment of blacks by the police and warned of the dangers. The report was generally dismissed as alarmist or biased. For their part the police were greatly concerned about the high level of street crime in Brixton, especially the number of muggings. In operation "Swamp 81" the police stepped up their "stop and search" tactics. This operation began on Monday, 6 April. By Friday, 10 April, the police had stopped, searched and questioned 943 people, half of them black. Of those searched, only 93 people were charged, mainly with minor offences.

The incident that led to the first violence is somewhat obscure, but it is clear that a week of "Swamp 81" had raised hostility to the police to new heights. Police Constable Stephen Margiotta, on routine patrol on Friday, 10 April, saw a young black man running away from two or three others. He tried to stop the fleeing men – reasonably suspecting a crime of

53 Bristol 1980: the police officer stands outside the burnt-out Lloyds bank in the St Paul's area of Bristol, following the riots on 3 April 1981. The riot erupted when police raided the "Black and White Club" used by the local Jamaican community.
▼

54 Brixton 1981: though a warning had appeared in the Bristol riots of 1980, the eruption of violence in Brixton still took the nation by surprise. In Bristol the police had withdrawn from the rioting area, but in Brixton the police engaged with the rioters.

violence – and found the young man bleeding from a stab wound. However, a crowd soon gathered and "rescued" the injured man, sending him to hospital in a minicab. A number of police vans arrived on the scene. The crowds threw bricks at them. The fighting continued until some older black people persuaded the crowd to disperse.

Trouble erupted again on Saturday afternoon, 11 April. Hundreds of people, young and old, black and white, were at a loose end in the Brixton market area. A number had been drinking, some had been smoking marijuana. The police began to question a black minicab driver whom they had seen tuck something in his socks. He explained that he was hiding his money. A crowd gathered, with much pushing and shoving. The police arrested a bystander,

pushing him into a police van. The crowd attacked the police van and rescued the prisoner. The fight had begun; it lasted late into Saturday night.

The original incidents involved black people, but many white youths soon showed that their sympathies lay with the blacks against the police. Crude fire bombs were made, doubtlessly based on techniques used in Northern Ireland. Much damage was done on that Saturday night. Private cars were pushed into the street and set alight; many police vehicles were overturned. Shop windows were smashed. Thieves from all over south London – mainly white – arrived to help themselves. On Sunday it began again; the pattern of destruction and looting was the same. In all, the riots lasted three days. The police at first decided that the rioting was the work of "outside agitators", but there was no evidence of this. The first Brixton riot was quite spontaneous.

Between 14 April and late June, the streets of Britain's cities were quiet, though many

61

following evening the police were again attacked with stones and bricks. By the Sunday evening seven-year-olds had joined the smashing and burning. On the Monday, the mobs turned to the burning of large buildings. C.S. gas was fired at rioters for the first time ever in England; the police also used cartridges which injured several rioters and bystanders. After over 200 policemen from other forces had been drafted in to Toxteth, violence temporarily subsided.

Over the next week there were "copycat" riots in other cities. On 8-9 July Moss Side in

55 The police, in fact, appear to have been the main target for the rioters and here we see a police van overturned and set on fire.

people in the inner cities were apprehensive. Trouble then broke out in late June in Peckham, south London. There was an apparently prearranged fight between black youths and skinheads at a Peckham fairground. Nearby, a Nigerian youth, not involved in the fight, was dragged out of a fish and chip shop and stabbed to death on the pavement. More violence occurred in south London following an incident on the night of 2-3 July, when petrol was poured through the letterbox of a house in Walthamstow in east London, and set alight. The wife of the householder, Mrs Khan, and their three small sons were burnt to death.

By coincidence, the night of 3 July saw the outbreak of far greater violence in the area known as Liverpool 8, or Toxteth. The initial incident was similar to those elsewhere. Police tried to arrest a black man on what they thought was a stolen motor bike. In fact, the bike was his own. His friends freed him and attacked the police with stones. On the

56 Liverpool, July 1981. Liverpool quickly followed Brixton into riot, and here the streets of Toxteth can be seen smouldering after a night of arson.

62

Manchester was the scene of violent disturbances. But the local police had already prepared a disciplined force to deal with disorder. Also, the police had a routine for getting in touch with local black leaders. The trouble was soon quelled. A small riot soon fizzled out in the Handsworth district of Birmingham at about the same time. Handsworth had the second largest concentration of black people, but a long tradition of "community policing" and careful consultation with black leaders enabled the police to prevent further trouble.

The second wave of Brixton riots erupted in July, on the weekend of 10-12. Two cars were burnt on the main road out of London, one of them a police car. The police raided and smashed up a row of houses occupied by blacks. This appeared to the black community to be an act of retaliation. The police said they were looking for bombs, although they had a drugs warrant. They found neither. Riots were reported all over Britain that weekend. There was trouble in Birmingham, Blackburn, Bradford, Derby, Leeds, Leicester and Wolverhampton. Petrol bombs were thrown in the Welsh mining valleys. How much the press distorted events is difficult to know, but every local reporter seemed intent on finding a riot.

The violence ended rather suddenly, and without any apparent reason at the end of July. The final incident occurred in Toxteth on a warm night on 28-29 July. Toxteth had been simmering since early July. With the start of the school holidays, children had taken to the streets looking for adventure. The police, expecting further trouble, were nervous and angry, according to a later report in *The Economist*. Around midnight on 28 July a police vehicle ran down a young white cripple. By most accounts, he was passing by, nothing to do with disturbances. The incident provoked further violence, but this and the news of his death – the only fatal casualty of the summer riot – was overshadowed in the media by the wedding of the Prince of Wales and Lady Diana Spencer the following morning.

Though each riot had its own particular causes, there were some common factors. The economic recession, especially rising unemployment, particularly affected the young, who formed a majority in all the riots. It was inner city areas where the rioting was worst. Over the last decade or more there has been a rapid decline in population in such areas, with a 30% fall in a number of cities since the early 1960s. Those who remained tended to include a high percentage of low paid and poorly educated people. Immigration rose in the 1950s and '60s. This has increased social tensions in some cities. Most of the riot areas had a significant immigrant community. The police appear to have been the major targets for violence. In the inner cities, the crime control methods of the police focused particularly on young blacks, and often seem to have offended the majority of the black population.

Two factors above all stand out as the cause of disturbances in 1981. The high level of youth unemployment is one. The high level of unemployment that hit most of Europe in the early 1980s coincided with the largest-ever generation of young people leaving school. Youth unemployment in Britain is higher than in most European countries except Italy. There are a number of reasons for this. Britain is the only European country without compulsory military service for teenagers. Also British teenagers' wages are a higher proportion of adult wages than in most countries in Europe. Sacking British workers is expensive because most are covered by redundancy payments. There is a strong tendency therefore for British firms to retain older workers rather than take on young ones. Moreover, the teenage population has risen fastest in the inner cities. Consequently unemployment is highest among the young and the black – and black youths are more likely than any other group to be unemployed.

Poor relations between the police and the black population in the inner cities was the second major factor in the riots. The police force is overwhelmingly white. In London, for example, at the time of the Brixton riots, there

57 Liverpool 1981. From the ground level a policeman, still carrying his riot shield, surveys a similar scene of arson and damage with burnt-out vehicles and wreckage strewn across the street.

were only 110 policemen or policewomen out of 24,000 who were other than white. In the 1970s the Metropolitan Police had made serious attempts to recruit black men and women, but with little success. Of those black people who tried to join the force, a number lacked the educational qualifications. Some who became policemen failed to serve for long. According to one article in *The Economist* "they met in the police stations a pattern of racial comment – at best thoughtless jokes, at worst open contempt – that made life intolerable".

The main conflict between the police and the black community had up to 1981 been the "SUS law", which enabled the police to stop

and search on suspicion. The police, and indeed communities in the inner cities, were worried about rising crime levels. "Mugging" was on the increase, and this involved young black people. The police tried to combat the increase in mugging by using their powers to stop and search suspects on the street, under the Vagrancy Act of 1834. It was the tactics of "Swamp 81" with its intensive stop and search which, as we have seen, provoked the first riots in Brixton in April 1981. Many of the police themselves in the capital were aware of the need to win over black communities, yet even after the first riots the incident of the police wrecking a row of black people's housing occurred.

Lord Scarman was appointed on 14 April 1981 to "inquire urgently into the serious disorder in Brixton on 10-12 April". Lord Scarman made recommendations on both the police and the wider social and economic issues. Recruitment of ethnic minorities into the police should be increased and there should be statutory liaison committees between the police and the communities they serve. Also, lay visitors should have the power to make random checks on suspects held in prison. The strongest plea made by Lord Scarman was for an attack on racial disadvantage:

Good policing will be of no avail unless we also tackle and eliminate basic flaws in our society. And if we succeed in eliminating racial prejudice from our society, it will not be difficult to achieve good policing.

In 1982 and '83 British cities were again quiet. Certain, though limited social measures, have been taken to improve some of the worst inner cities and greater emphasis has been put on community policing. But a significant proportion of Scarman's recommendations have not been carried out. Moreover those local authorities with the worst social problems are those which are being financially squeezed, and may lose some of their financial independence in a rate-capping bill, proposed by the Conservative government. By 1984 therefore, there was no great momentum towards urban renewal. Policing may have improved, but the social and economic causes of the riots have scarcely been tackled, let alone eliminated. There is no hope that the massive social programme adopted by the Americans at a period of economic growth in the 1960s, and which helped to eliminate racial disadvantage, will be followed in Britain, especially in the harsh climate of the 1980s.

The Miners' Dispute, 1984

In the spring of 1984 a number of miners came out on strike in protest at the Coal Board

58 Miners' dispute, 1984. Police force back NUM pickets near Llanwern steelworks. In the first six months of 1984 the miners' strike produced some of the worst industrial violence seen for many decades. This scene was only one of many which appeared in newspapers and on television screens.
▼

wanting to close pits that were losing money. Soon some two-thirds of mine workers were on strike, but in the absence of a national ballot the remaining third continued to work. Pickets, sometimes numbering thousands, tried to prevent their fellow miners from continuing to work. The result was some of the worst industrial violence of this century, as pickets clashed with police who had been organized on a massive scale to prevent pickets closing down working mines. Scores of violent clashes appeared daily on television screens and in the newspapers. By September 1984 two pickets had already been killed and a police spokesman claimed that the level of violence was worse than the rioting in the inner cities in 1981. This is probably an impossible comparison to make: between the spontaneous, enormously destructive riots of 1981, which were nevertheless very limited in length, and a form of traditional working-class protest which has assumed a more violent dimension. What seems certain is that the clashes mark a new level of industrial violence in the twentieth century, and set a dangerous precedent for future industrial disputes.

Date List

1710	Sacheverell riots
1715	Riot Act
1768	Wilkes riots
1780	Gordon riots
1811	Luddite riots
1815	Corn Laws passed
1816	Spa Fields Meeting
1819	Peterloo Massacre
1820	Cato Street Conspiracy
1831	Bristol riots over rejection of Reform Bill
1831-32	Swing riots
1835	Municipal Corporations Act
1839	County Police Act
1867	Franchise extended to include many urban workers
1868	Election riot at Blackburn
1872	Secret Ballot Act
1883	Corrupt Practices Act
1884	Further extension of the franchise to include many rural workers
1887	Trafalgar Square disturbances
1919	Strike on Clydeside
1932	Violent disturbances at Birkenhead over unemployment
1934	Meeting of British Union of Fascists at Olympia
1958	Notting Hill riots
1972	Demonstrations in Red Lion Square, London
1974	Shewsbury pickets
1977	Lewisham riots
1981	Riots in Brixton and Toxteth
1984	Industrial violence in the miners' strike

Glossary

Chartism The first working-class political movement, which, in 1839, 1842 and 1848 presented the People's Charter to parliament, demanding, among other things, votes for all men and secret ballots.

Collective bargaining by riot the idea that many riots, especially in the eighteenth century, were almost a form of negotiation by workers, in the absence of the necessary organization to "bargain collectively".

Dearth shortages, especially food.

Dissenters those Protestants who did not belong to the Established Church of England.

Jacobin a member of the political club of the French Revolution, founded in May 1784 and later led by Robespierre. It then became a general term for anyone who supported the French Revolution.

Means test a process introduced in the 1930s whereby, once national insurance payments ran out after 26 weeks, applicants for benefits had to declare all sources of income from other members of the family, or any savings held before any money was given to them.

Municipal Corporations Act a wide-ranging measure of local reform, including a widening of the franchise in local government and the obligation on boroughs to establish a police force.

Nonconformist Protestants who did not belong to the Established Church, and as a result suffered certain social and political disadvantages up to the early nineteenth century.

Pocket borough a borough which before 1832 could send two MPs to Parliament, despite the fact that it had such a small number of votes that it was under the control of, i.e. in the pocket of, a single powerful landowner or urban dignitary. Such boroughs were abolished in 1832.

Popery the term used by many Protestants to descibe Catholicism.

Presbyterianism a form of dissent or nonconformity. The Presbytarians were one of the most powerful dissenting groups in late seventeenth-century England.

Rate-capping the process whereby the Thatcher Government (elected 1983) punishes local authorities who overspend, by withdrawing some money from its rate support grant.

Sabbath-breaking not observing the Sabbath as a holy day. Ever since the seventeenth century, certain English Protestants have placed great emphasis on keeping Sunday "The Sabbath" as a day reserved primarily for religious worship. People who attempt to do other things, such as trading or playing sport, are considered "Sabbath-breakers".

Spenceans a small group of extreme left wing radicals led by Dr Watson and Arthur Thistlewood who were prepared to use violence in support of parliamentary reform after 1815.

Syndicalism a political and economic theory advocating the use of general strikes and force by the workers. This idea gained support among British Trades Unionists in the early part of this century.

Truck-system a practice, used in the nineteenth century, of paying workers in goods rather than money. This was much resented, especially as it was open to abuse.

Turnout getting workers out of factories to join a strike.

Suggestions for Further Reading

E.J. Hobsbaum and G. Rudé,
Captain Ewing,
Penguin, 1973

G. Holmes,
'The Sacheverell Riots'
Past and Present, 1972

F.C. Mather,
Chartism,
Historical Association pamphlet, 1965

D. Richter
Riotous Victorians
Ohio University Press, 1975

G. Rudé
The Crowd in History,
Wiley, 1964

P. Searby,
The Chartists,
Then and There series,
Longman, 1967

P.F. Speed,
Police and Prisons,
Then and There series,
Longman, 1968

J. Stevenson,
Popular Disturbances in England,
Longman, 1979

J. Stevenson and R. Quinault,
*Popular Protest and Public Order: Six Studies
in British History 1790-1920,*
Allen and Unwin, 1974

J. Steven and C. Cook,
The Slump,
Quartet Books, 1979

E.P. Thompson,
The Making of the English Working Classes
Second edition, Penguin, 1968

E.P. Thompson,
'The Moral Economy of the English Crowd in
the Eighteenth Century'
Past and Present 50, 1971

R.F. Wearmouth,
*Methodism and the Common Profile of the
Eighteenth Century,*
Epworth, 1945

Index